The Tunisian Cookbook

A Celebration of Healthy Red Cuisine from Carthage to Kairouan

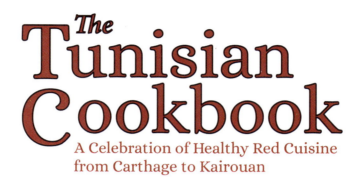

The Tunisian Cookbook

A Celebration of Healthy Red Cuisine
from Carthage to Kairouan

Hafida Ben Rejeb Latta

This book is dedicated to my Mother Cherifa, my Grandmother Rekaya and all the women of Tunisia who have taken care to pass their culinary passions to the next generations with their experience of healthy eating.

Acknowledgements

No book can be completed without help from lots of people and I would like to thank all those who were generous with their contributions of recipes: My aunt Fatma, My sister Zohra, my cousin Moufida Ferchichi, my cousin's daughter Samah Ben Rejeb of the restaurant in Kairouan 'Espace Al Rachid', my neighbour Jamila, my friends: Amel Kechrid, Janet, Rabia, Jackie, Nargis, Naima, Alia, Monique, Chefs: Mohamed Salah, Rafram Chaddad and Mohsen Said and of course Mother and Grandmother. Thanks go, too, to our sponsor CHO olive oil company. Their generosity of spirit advances the dissemination of the healthy and delicious Tunisian cuisine. My thanks are not restricted to the provision of recipes but also to Ridha Kechrid and Samah Ben Rejeb for information about Arwa and Pliny the Elder respectively.

This book would not having seen the light of day without the support of H.E. Ambassador of Tunisia in London, Nabil Ben Khedher and I am in his debt. From our first meeting he has been a great source of inspiration and encouragement. This attitude of his is extended to all our community in the UK. My deepest thanks go to my publisher Max Scott for his patience, support, and skills - a charming perfectionist with amazing editorial know-how to promote the efforts of mere writers. And to my husband David for his moral support. He has always been there for me. I have been very blessed with support, encouragement and belief in me. I thank them all from the bottom of my heart.

The Publishers would also like to thank CHO Group and the British-Tunisian Society for their support.

The Tunisian Cookbook
A Celebration of Healthy Red Cuisine from Carthage to Kairouan
by Hafida Ben Rejeb Latta
ISBN 978-1-914325-08-3

© Hafida Ben Rejeb Latta 2022

Published by Nomad Publishing in 2022
Email: info@nomad-publishing.com
www.nomad-publishng.com
Design: Martin Humphreys
Photographic credits: Pocket Creatives
Printed in India by Imprint Press
Chapter opener images: the renowned Tunisian painter and sculptor, Zubeir Turki, with thanks to the Ministry of Culture
Special thanks are due to Hatem and Amina at Sidi Bou Restaurant in London for their generous support in preparing the recipes presented in the photographs here.

All rights are reserved. No part of this publication may be reproduced, stored in a retrieval system or transmitted in any form or by any means, electronic, mechanical, photographic or otherwise, without prior permission of the copyright holder.
CIP Data: A catalogue for this book is available from the British Library

CONTENTS

Introduction   7

The Cordoba Calendar   9

Chronology   11

Foreword   15

A Note on Ingredients   28

The A to Z of Tunisian Spices   29

Healthy Cuisine   30

Dishes for Special Occasions   33
    Shorbat Frik *36*, Kairouan Makroudh *39*, Mrayish *41*, The Bey's Baklava *42*, Zlebia *44*

Couscous   47
    Fish couscous *50*, Chicken couscous *52*, Lamb couscous *53*

Briks & Savoury Pastries   55
    Egg briks *59*, Chicken briks *60*, Vegetable cake *61*

Tajins & Maaquoudas   63
    Chicken Tajin *66*, Tajin with Malsouqa *68*, , Potato Maaquouda *70*, Cauliflower Maaquouda *71*

Soups   73
    Whole chicken and vegetable soup *76*, Fish soup from the Tunisian Sahel *79*, Fish Broudou *80*, Barkoukech *81*, Borghol *82*, White dried bean soup *83*, Lablabi *84*, Sfax Hlelem *87*

Pasta Dishes   89
    Spaghetti with Lamb *92*, Macaroni in the oven *93*, Sousse Beef and Tomato Macaroni *95*

Salads   97
    Slata Mechouia *100*, Slata Tunisia *102*, Slatit Blankit *105*, Omok

Houria *107*, Radish Salad *108*, Anchovy salad *109*, Anchovy salad *109*, Fricassée *111*, Slatat Fondouq El Ghalla *113*, La Goulette octopus salad *114*

Fish Dishes   **117**
Poisson Complet *121*, La Goulette fish cakes *122*, Le Kram Fish Stew *123*, Stuffed Squid *124*, Octopus with Garlic *125*

Meat Dishes   **127**
Kairouan stiffed chicken *130*, Tunis Walnut Chicken *132*, Kairouan Chicken with Almonds Sauce *133*, Rice in the Oven with Chicken *134*, Marinated lamb cutlets *135*, Leg of Lamb with Artichokes *136*, Kifta Bil Salsa *138*, Kairouan Winter Dish, Lamb with Spinach *140*, Stuffed Beef Sirloin *142*, Tahfifa *143*

Vegetables Dishes   **145**
Kafteji *147*, Stuffed Artichoke *148*, Nabeul Aubergine *149*, Standard Chakchouka *151*, Stuffed tomatoes *153*, Beja Chakchouka *153*, Potatoes with Onion and Herbs *154*, Kairouan Potato Kifta *155*, Kairouan Koucha *157*

Sweets, Puddings & Drinks   **159**
Rfisa *163*, Pistachio Custard *164*, Tunis Almond Cake *164*, Apple Doughnuts *165*, Qutayef *166*, Sousse Fresh Melon *167*, Samsar *169*, Laklouka from Sfax *170*, Mhalbiya *171*, Ghraiba *173*, Zriga *173*, Mint tea with pine nuts *175*, Lemonade *176*, Rosata *177*

Pickles & Breads   **178**
Hot pepper *180*, Eggplant *180*, Turnips *181*, Breads *182*, Kairouan bread *185*, Kairouan bread *185*, Mabsout *187*

Glossary   **188**

Further Reading   **189**

Index   **190**

INTRODUCTION

Dr. Simon Poole

It is often said that Tunisia is the jewel of North Africa. The verdant fertile valleys, breath-taking views across the crystal-clear waters of the Mediterranean and extraordinarily well-preserved monuments of past civilizations are indeed testament to Tunisia's uniquely alluring geography and singular place in history.

Yet it is not just the beauty of the land, the energy of bustling modern cities or the quiet of small rustic villages which appear unchanged in centuries that makes this country so special. The welcoming smiles and generous hospitality of its people bear witness to the importance of breaking bread together with family, friends or visitors and enjoying the conviviality of sharing fresh, local, seasonal food with old stories, vibrant conversation and laughter.

The cuisine of Tunisia is perhaps one of the greatest undiscovered treasures of the Mediterranean, and reflects the country's proud heritage of embracing and assimilating the exotic foods and tastes of other cultures. From the Phoenician sailors who brought the olive tree and Spanish explorers returning with tomatoes from the New World, to traders who introduced the herbs and spices from the Middle East so valued by ancient physicians for their health-giving properties, Tunisia has always been a melting pot of societies and food traditions. Delicate flavours of garden vegetables contrast with pungent seasoning, in harmony with the ubiquitous regional extra virgin olive oil from ancient cultivars that are now the subject of contemporary research rebeefing profound benefits for health at the heart of the Mediterranean diet.

From Carthage to Kairouan takes us on a remarkable and absorbing journey to unveil the secrets of the diverse and magnificent culinary expression of Tunisia. Hafida, our eminently qualified guide, brings her intimate knowledge of local recipes passed down from one generation to the next, and shares with us exquisite dishes, describing the relationship of the delicious combinations of ingredients with the deep-rooted customs and the history of the region. As we accompany Hafida to explore and celebrate the tastes of her homeland, our senses become alive to the aromas and enticing flavours of the homes of our hosts as we are invited across the threshold. We might imagine the busy sounds of the kitchen mingling with the call to prayer. And we hear the stories of the red cuisine of Tunisia. These are Hafida's stories. These are the stories of the people of Tunisia. These are beautiful and captivating tales that reach out and connect with us so deeply to enlighten and enrich our world.

Dr. Simon Poole
March 2022

THE CORDOBA CALENDAR

'All the world's a stage,
And all the men and women merely players:
They have their exits and their entrances.'
Shakespeare - As You Like It, Act II, Scene vii

Shakespeare's quote applies to cultures and nations just as much as to people. When the spotlight shines on you, it is time to perform to the whole world. Arab civilization on the Iberian Peninsula was one such moment, as it reached a peak of human achievement on many fronts, in disciplines as varied as astronomy, agriculture and medicine. Armed with experience of market gardening in desert conditions and expertise with irrigation systems the Arabs turned Andalusia into a land of milk and honey.

Around AD 961 Recemund, a Christian native of Cordoba, capped a successful career as a civil servant with a later appointment as Bishop of Elvira (the early name for the city of Granada). Recemund is the initiator of the Córdoba Calendar, a comprehensive register of agricultural products and their uses in Islamic Andalusia. Some of the products mentioned in the Calendar were no doubt already present in Spain, but at least half were previously unknown to Christian Europe. Since conquered by the Arabs in AD 711, Andalusia had clearly undergone an agricultural revolution.

These products improved peoples' health. Hard *(durum)* wheat, the main constituent of pasta, grows in drier conditions than soft wheat and stores for a prodigiously long time because of its low water content. Al-Razi (d.955) tells that around Toledo it could safely be stored for upwards of 60 years and was passed from father to son like other inherited property. This crop clearly helped to stave off the threat of famine. Prosperity promoted earlier marriage, larger families, diversification, opportunity and leisure. There were luxuries such as textiles, ivories, ceramics, cosmetics, metal-work, fine wood- and leather-work. Linen from Andalusia was exported as far as Egypt. A wide range of silks was much sought after. From the 1540s musical instruments became a speciality of Seville, and paper came from Europe's first paper factory in Jativa a century or so later.

The Cordoba Calendar is a thorough study of the seasons of the year, and how climate and astrology affect farming and agriculture. It describes when seeds must be sown, and crops harvested. Agriculture shapes the foundations of human societies. When food becomes more plentiful people benefit from a richer diet. They grow healthier and more creative. At this point cuisine is born, and once discovered it is rarely lost because it enters a nation's DNA. The Calendar also mentions festivities and their links to the special foods eaten to celebrate them.

Controversy can surround judgments on what crops were introduced when in what region. The claims made in the Cordoba Calendar are based on written evidence and crops likely to have grown in Andalusia prior to the Arab invasion have been omitted. Some seventy identifiable crops are covered by the Calendar. The following fruits, vegetables, and herbs were brought, on the balance of probability, by the Muslim invaders to Andalusia:-

Fruits: blueberries, dates, figs, bananas, Barbary figs, several varieties of grape and melons, mulberries, peaches, pine nuts, pistachios, pomegranates, quinces, watermelons.

Vegetables: aubergines, broad beans, carrots, Swiss chard, fennel, garlic, radishes, sugar-cane.

Other crops: almonds, aniseed, saffron, safflower, cotton, henna, jasmine, mustard-seed, rice, sumac, thyme, walnuts, wheat, poppies, irises and chrysanthemums, sugar-cane.

The Calendar also listed proteins added to their diet by eating pigeon, peacock, partridge, ostrich, mullet, sardines and fish roe.

The Arabs ate the fruits raw, made jams, dried them and made them into drinks. Their farm workers had access to an instruction book telling them when to plant or sow, harvest or prune their crops.

Most of their breads had no yeast. Their animals provided milk, which was used for cooking and pastries. This amounted to a veritable cornucopia of products new to Latin Christendom. Most of these crops and products must have first grown in the Maghreb. This includes Tunisia, as an actor then on 'the world stage' in Shakespeare's quote, while the produce listed for Andalusia also entered into Tunisia's DNA.

CHRONOLOGY

World Events	Era/Year	Events in Tunisia
Pyramids of Giza built	2580-04 BC	
Trojan Wars	1194-84 BC	
	814 BC	Carthage founded by the Phoenicians (Introduction of olive trees)
Rome founded	753 BC	
Alexander the Great, King of Macedonia	336 BC	
Dies in Babylon	323 BC	
	264-241 BC	First Punic War, which Rome wins
	221 BC	Hannibal elected leader of Carthage
	218 BC	Hannibal crosses the Alps
	216 BC	Hannibal defeats Romans at Cannae
	205 BC	Battle of Zama south of Carthage ends Second Punic War with Hannibal's defeat
	183 BC	Death of Hannibal in exile in Libyssa, near the Bosporus Straits (Turkey)
	146 BC	Romans destroy Carthage and colonize Ifrikiya*
----------------	----------------	----------------
Launch of Christian era	AD 27	
	AD 70	Pliny the Elder writes in admiration of Gabes Oasis
	AD 155-220	Tertullian (born in Carthage) - the first theologian to coin the idea of the Holy Trinity
	AD 200-410	Roman occupation of Ifrikiya*, making it its bread basket
	AD 311-314	"Tunisian" Pope Melchiades reigns in Rome
Rome destroyed by Visigoths and Vandals. Western Roman empire collapses	AD 410	Vandals settle in North Africa and are Christianized
"Al-Hijra": The Prophet Mohammad flees from Mecca to Medina, marking the start of the Islamic Calendar	AD 622	
	AD 670	Uqba Ibn Nafi establishes a military camp in Kairouan in the name of the Caliph and builds the Great Mosque
	AD 702-788	Kairouan becomes the Capital of North Africa the centre of Islam
Arabs from Ifrikiya rule all of Sicily and Malta	AD 827-902	

* Ifrikiya was the term adopted by Arab historians from AD800 - 909 to refer to what is today Tunisia and eastern Algeria.

World Events	Era/Year	Events in Tunisia
Recemund's Calendar listed Umayyad crops grown in Andalusia, many of them for the first time in Europe	961	
Norman Conquest of England	1066	
Norman Conquest of Sicily begins	1091	
Latin Christian forces capture Jerusalem in the First Crusade	1099	
	1150	Ifrikiya resists Norman Invasion. Originally a Berber settlement, Tunis becomes the capital of the region under the rule of Al Mohad and Hafsid, and Berber rule continues, albeit interrupted, until 1570.
	1270	French King Louis IX dies in Tunis ending his Crusading career followed by a trade agreement with France and Sicily Other trade agreements with Venice, Pisa, Genoa and Navarre The Bardo Aqueducts built in 1276
	1332	Birth of Ibn Khaldun in Tunis, a famous historian and social scientist. Dies in Cairo in 1406
The Black Death spreads from Asia all over Europe	1346-53	
	1421	Mohamed Ibn Arefa (1315-99) becomes Imam of Zaytuna Mosque, which now takes over from Kairouan as the centre of Islam in Ifriqia.
Medici rule in Florence, presiding over the Renaissance	1432-92	Peace and trade agreement between Florence and Hafsid Tunisia of Abu Fares Abd al-A'ziz
First printing press in Europe	1440	
Moors expelled from Spain, Columbus lands in America, The Age of Inquisition begins	1492	Muslim refugees from Andalusia flee to *Ifriqia*
Rule of Suleiman the Magnificent; apogee of Ottoman power	1520-66	
Kheireddine Barbarossa appointed admiral of Ottoman fleet	1533	
English King Henry VIII - Reformation; leaves the Catholic church and disbands monasteries	1536-41	
	1574	Tunis falls under Ottoman suzarainty until the 1870s
	1607	80,000 Muslims are exiled from Spain settle in Tunisia
Galileo sights four of Jupiter's moons	1610	
Pilgrim ship 'Mayflower' reaches Cape Cod	1620	
	1705-1957	Reign of the Ottoman-appointed Beys in Tunis
Acts of Union unites Scotland and England	1707	
Seven-Years' War expands British colonial possessions	1756-1763	

World Events	Era/Year	Events in Tunisia
Catherine the Great of Russia promotes spread of smallpox vaccination	1768	
American Declaration of Independence	1776	
French Revolution	1789	
Europe industrializes via railways	1820s	
France colonizes Algeria	1834	
French protectorate follows invasion of Algeria	1848	
Opening of the Suez Canal	1869	
	1875	Foundation of famous Sadiki College
	1881	French troops occupy Tunisia
Henry Ford's first car factory	1893	
First mechanized flight by the Wright brothers in the USA	1903	
World War I	1914-18	
	1920	Foundation of the Destour Party
	1929	Taher Haddad publishes 'Our Women in Sharia and Society' defending womens' rights
	1934	Habib Bourguiba founds the secular Neo Destour Party
World War II	1939-45	
	1941-44	Tunisia becomes a zone of conflict as part of the Second World War
India and Pakistan win independence from British Colonial control	1947	
	1956	Tunisia becomes independent
	1959	First Tunisian general election
	1961	Habib Bourguiba visits USA
Algeria gains its independence	1962	
	1964	Tunisian land and property reform
First manned flight lands on the moon	1969	
	1979	UNESCO designates the Medina of Tunis as a World Heritage Site.
	1981	1981 - First multi-party parliamentary elections. President Bourguiba's party wins by a landslide.
	1987	Prime Minister Zine El Abidine Ben Ali has President Bourguiba declared mentally unfit to rule and takes power himself.
	2011	Arab Spring starts in Tunisia

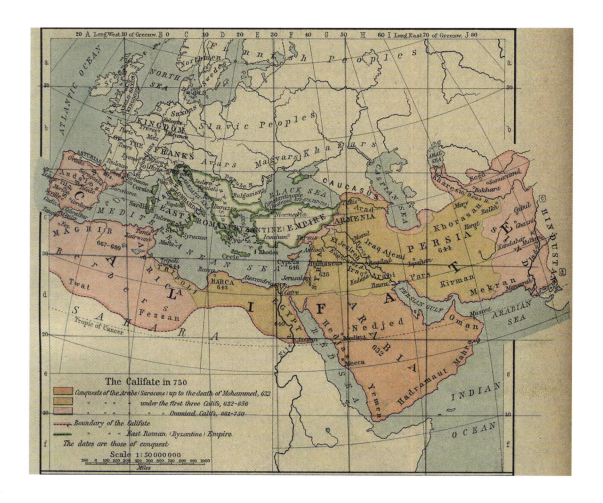

*In this archive image from The Historical Atlas of 1923 **(above)**, we see a presentation of the Islamic Empire's expansion at its fullest extent in the last years of the Ummayad Caliphate, AD 750. Having swept across the Maghreb from Damascus in Syria to Cordoba in Spain, the Empire finally ruptured into two parts, with the Eastern side falling to the successor Abbasid Caliphate. The traces the migrant empire left in passing through Tunisia were to prove to be indelible and survive in the national cuisine to this day.*

FOREWORD

'There under the very high palm tree grows the olive tree.
At the foot of the olive tree grows the fig tree.
At the foot of the fig tree the pomegranate.
And at the foot of the pomegranate tree wheat is planted.
Then the vegetables grow, then the herbs,
All in the same year,
Each one shaded under another.'

Description of the Oasis of Gabes in 70-72 AD by Pliny the Elder from his *Natural History*

The world today is in need of cheer as it negotiates its passage through the pandemic. So let me tell you how the women of Tunisia pulled their families through difficult times. They claimed the family home for themselves. Their home is no prison, as is often perceived by others. It is the centre of their physical and emotional world, with the kitchen as its hub. They turned it into their laboratory, experimenting with recipes, adding new ones to their menus. It became the link between the fields that produced the ingredients and the table around which the family gathers to relax and enjoy moments of special delight.

It also became the birthplace of hospitality as an art form. They believed, moreover, that a healthy diet protected them from illness and rewarded them for their open and friendly attitude to the world. Even today, many visitors to Tunisia are surprised to find smiling faces greeting them. But it comes as no surprise, when one realizes that this welcome has long been taught. A game called 'hostesses and visitors' is played by children from an early age. In it they compete against each other with words of welcome and the right intonations, gestures and smiles, as their parents encourage and judge the performance. With this game to inspire them Tunisian people learn the value of hospitality from an early age. They work out their priorities, and vow to nurture life itself within loving families.

The Mediterranean world was once a wild place, and raids and skirmishes were the main cause of suffering in that land. They destroyed many homes and families, until people found a solution. It was like walking into a lion's den,

*Olive trees, and olive oil **(left and opposite, respectively)** lie at the very heart of Tunisian life and cuisine.*

Foreword

but when the men-folk went unarmed to treat fighters like guests, smilingly offering them hot, minty drinks and cakes laced with honey, they found that visitors do not stay hostile forever. Eventually they all go home. That was how, with a stroke of good luck, the toll of violence began to reduce. People began to come in peace, to learn what was cultivated in Tunisian fields and how animals were husbanded locally. We never forgot the magical power of hospitality and how it had saved us.

The first notable visitors were refugees from the ancient Phoenician city-state of Tyre, led by its exiled Princess Dido (Elissa). On the day she arrived on our shores we sent her the usual cakes and drinks and quickly learnt her tragic story. Her jealous brother had murdered her beloved husband and would have killed her, too, had she not fled to sea with as many of her household as would accompany her into uncertain exile. Upon her landing in North Africa the local Berber chieftain agreed to cede to her as much land as could be covered by a single ox hide. The resourceful Dido cut the hide into very thin strips and laid them end to end until they encircled the hill she wanted for her settlement. That was how the foundations of the city were fixed and a great Carthaginian Empire was launched. With Dido's help the city prospered and she was made Queen. She rewarded her people by sending home for an army of the strangest little plants and teaching their cultivation. Nobody believed her when she told them they produced holy oil and lived for ever, but she was right. She called them olive trees. Not long after that a neighbouring King Larbas, proposed either marriage or war between their peoples. She wanted neither, because she loved her people and remained loyal to the memory of her husband. Soon women were flocking to her camp to offer sympathies. Sadly she remained broken-hearted and did not live for long enough for us to thank her properly. Later everyone agreed that respect for hospitality and the custom of eating quietly together in the family was the best recipe for a healthy life. Dido had left a lasting legacy.

The moral of this story is that, now as then, we must all champion life itself and protect our families from every possible threat. The act of sharing food together is one of the very best ways to achieve this goal. Tunisian folk have lived by this belief through wars, hardships and major switches of religion. They remain constantly among the most open and hospitable people on Earth. This book hopes to spread the message that, if women keep to this pathway and men either support them wholeheartedly, or, better, join their partners in preparing the family meal, the jungle that lies outside the home becomes a safer place and mindless violence begins to melt away. Great powers for good reside in the kitchen, because cooking is love made visible.

The olive tree lies at the heart of Mediterranean cooking. Its roots, trunk, branches, twigs, leaves and fruits, all promote the healthy living brought by Dido's people. The wood is turned into artefacts and the foliage is often applied for medicinal purposes, while the fruits became oil for lamplight, cooking, and today, appetizers and cosmetics. Without roots and trunks a tree cannot grow leaves and without supportive dietary roots societies can wither, too. Food and drink are life-sustaining. But this book is not just about sustenance. It starts there, but must extend to culture, family life and the memory banks they fill. Food feeds physically and emotionally. In the end it helps to shape our identity.

The strong roots of the olive tree set Tunisian cookery within the ambit of Mediterranean cuisine, which it also strengthens. It has developed through the same three stages as other countries; from a base of survival skills, through new eating habits developed by agriculture and food preparation, to the modern era of scientific and technological progress. As and when piped water, refrigeration, electricity and internet access become available to equip the domestic kitchens of the age of science, improved eating habits will be reachable by all Tunisian homes. Better health, better educational skills and longer, happier lives may at least become an option to which every household can aspire. Together coastal Tunisia and its olive groves watched invasions come and go, while both families and trees remained firmly grounded, producing healthy food and living at peace with the neighbours. Further inland the Tunisian 'Deglet Noor' date is harvested in the southern oases from October to December. An established annual treat in the food markets of the United Kingdom, dates add a sweet and fibre-rich mouthful

to the Christmas table. Small and almost translucent compared to other varieties, it has been cultivated for several thousand years in the south of Tunisia and makes a significant contribution to the diet of oasis dwellers.

Tunisia is situated around the mid-point of North Africa's Mediterranean coast, not far below the southern tip of Sicily. For the past sixty-five years, since its separation from France 20th March 1956, it has been an independent republic. Before that it was governed by outsiders. By African standards it is neither a big country, nor a very populous one. Most people live in northern cities and towns along a coastal strip, of relatively well watered land. Its earliest inhabitants were of Berber origin. Formerly nomadic they retain a special attachment to the soil and to their own language and customs. In this way the foundations of Tunisian culture were laid down by the original Bedouin inhabitants of the Atlas Mountains. They may have adopted Islam and developed a passion for motorized transport, but their own language is still spoken; many dress as their ancestors did, while their women-folk dress and wear the same jewels as their forebears. This display of granite-

*In a picture painted by the French artist Pierre-Narcisse Baron Guérin in 1815 **(above)**, the Trojan hero Aeneas tells Dido of the Trojan War.*

like durability, versatility and strength has provided the roots to nurture Tunisian culture.

Appropriately the signature dish, for Tunisia and the whole of North Africa, is couscous. And it was a Berber creation. Its unique ingredient, made from durum wheat, is its semoule (a farinaceous paste with a consistency a little less refined than flour, producing a savoury taste comparable to the difference between brown sugar and caster sugar). I believe it should be described as the main ingredient of one of the world's first pasta dishes. My hope is that, when you try it, you will agree with these claims. Couscous has other unique qualities. It lends itself to domestic production. It preserves grain better, and is more easily transported than flour. On the table it becomes as versatile as rice is to curry, or as the potato is to stews. That is why the dish has thrived and survived down the centuries. Its transfer into a national dish for all three Maghreb nations has helped to sustain the health and distinctive culture of these inhabitants throughout their history.

Another wonder of Tunisian cuisine lies in how closely its roots match the contrasting soils and climatic conditions of North Africa; how its staple foods echo the strength of the olive tree's distinctively hardwood trunk; and how so many of its branches have been grafted from other Mediterranean lands and sustain the essential crops and fruits to bring the next generation to fruition. These precious strengths will protect Tunisian society into the future. This realization determines the shape of our narrative. No Tunisian cookbook will be complete without sharing some insight into Tunisia's strong traditions of hospitality.

'The Tunisian Cookbook' is the chosen title of a book which aims to record the progressive additions to Tunisian tables and the national diet down the centuries. Both Carthage and Kairouan were once capital cities, but the torch has long since passed to Tunis. Tunisian cuisine is called the Red Cuisine. This refers not to the colour of its flag, but to the fact that lots of its dishes end up looking predominantly red from the presence of tomatoes, cayenne pepper, watermelon, sweet red peppers and *harissa*, all of them rich in vitamins, antioxidants and other nutrients. Of course, neither the chosen recipes nor the plates that grace Tunisian tables are all red – our selection has rejected the tyranny of excluding the rest of the rainbow, but still celebrates the recurring red hue which predominates in so many classical Tunisian dishes.

Tunisian diet fits comfortably within the five points of a star, with olive oil occupying the top spot. On the left side are vegetables, the queen of which is the tomato (for all that it is technically a fruit). The right side accommodates cereals, of which wheat is its leader, essential for breads, couscous, pastas and cakes. The two grounded points represent animals, led by the lamb heading the flock on the one hand; with fish and seafood on the other. This metaphorical star matches the one we see on the Tunisian national flag today.

John Tolan in 'On the Shoulders of Giants' writes:
'Trade is inseparable from political, diplomatic, and military relations. The mingling of people and goods travelling back and forth across the Mediterranean was accompanied by a mingling of ideas, technologies, and texts – institutions, and tools of the merchants and sailors – whether banking instruments, contracts, funduqs, compasses, or portulans – modified them to fit their own need and culture, and perfected them when necessary'.

The prosperity of Carthage attracted envy and interference from the next wave of visitors. They were the Romans, who after a series of fierce wars, destroyed Carthage and turned the land into the 'bread-basket' of their growing empire. Centuries later this empire crumbled when exhausted African soils ceased to yield their crops, mainly of wheat. Only some wonderfully preserved Roman ruins are left to attest to this early European presence in Tunisia. Amidst these ruins the eating habits of the day were recorded in vivid mosaic form. Roman hunters filled their cooking pots with meats, poultry and fish, while breads baked in their ovens. Delicious meats and vegetables were roasted in olive oil and washed down with wine. Some of the deepest roots of today's Mediterranean diet can be found in Tunisia as history dawned.

The most dramatic change to life in North Africa was the arrival of Islam from the East. Its introduction and spread from Cairo to the Atlantic was rapid and, if confrontation was not absent, it ended rapidly. Tunisia had, after all, followed Rome from pagan gods

Today the ruins of once great Carthage (above) stand on the shores of the Mediterranean as testament to a city that once threatened the very existence of the might of Rome itself.

to Christianity. Now its inhabitants were treated leniently as 'people of the book' while they adapted to the mosque. At this point important dietary habits changed to accommodate new feasts and disciplines. They reoriented Tunisian society in an easterly direction and a new range of fruits, vegetables and spices were brought to the table. Consensus on the list of products coming from the East for the first time is not easy to reach, but the putative bounty includes:-

• Fruits: Citrus fruits, Melons, Pomegranates and Apricots;
• Vegetables: aubergines, squash, sweet and hot peppers, Swiss chard and okra;
• Spices: Sesame and many Oriental spices;
• Other: Sugar, Almonds, Pistachios and chickpeas,

It is now time to talk about the Holy City, itself. Kairouan, (its name comes from the root-word for 'caravan'), was the military base built by Uqba ibn Nafih the leader of the first Muslim army to reach Ifrikiya (the Roman and Arab name for North Africa), across the Libyan desert in AD 670. A prosperous city with luxuriant gardens and olive groves emerged from the military camp, comparable in size and wealth to Basra and Kufa in the east, and launched a golden age reminiscent of Carthage in its prime. In the medieval period it was considered the fourth holiest city in Islam after Mecca, Medina and Jerusalem, a status proudly remembered in the present day. Kairouan was blessed with a plentiful supply of underground water, so that the city was generously provided with wells that rarely ran dry. But on the surface a climate of desert extremes prevailed. In high summer, when the heat drove everyone to shelter as best they could, the rich abandoned the city for the cooling breezes of coastal Sousse. In the depths of winter the setting sun plunged the men-folk deep into their enfolding *burnouses* in an effort to keep warm, while the women and children huddled close to tiny charcoal-burning clay pots. But worst of all was the fact that winter and summer seasons reached out to each other, so that the citizens passed rapidly from one extreme of temperature to the next. The seasons of autumn and spring, so jubilantly welcomed by English poets, are short. Today it is known that this curse resulted from over-intensive farming practices, which accelerated the northward advance of desert sands.

The new capital housed one of the most prestigious mosques on the continent of Africa. It included an embryonic university that specialized both in Islamic thought and in the secular sciences, such as the new algebra, astronomy, botany, medicine and a famous hospital. Kairouan established a Muslim peace in the Maghreb and dealt harmoniously with its several communities. It became a land of *convivencia*, in which the various religious communities 'of the book' lived at peace together. The first Jewish settlers arrived at the end of the seventh century. By the early eleventh century the city boasted a prosperous business community and the growing university attracted teachers from around the Muslim world. Jewish scholars also contributed to the high repute of the university and earned the privilege of teaching within the walls of the mosque.

The most enduring particularity of the city is its adherence to the Holy Koran, which in turn commands everyone to respect all three religions 'of the Book'. As a result the city housed a synagogue which remained active until the late 1960s. It was situated close to our house. On Saturdays, the Jewish Sabbath, the women of my family and their female neighbours would clamber across our flat-roofed houses to watch the service from above the synagogue and join in the happy atmosphere it generated. The Jewish community had also brought its cooking skills to the city. Their dishes were added to the city's rich mix of culinary styles. Perhaps because it stands between two climatic zones, of coastal plain filled with olive trees and the date palms of the desert oases, Kairouan never claimed to be the nation's culinary centre, but it still specializes in dishes to mark the feasts and holy days of the Muslim calendar. A section of this book is dedicated to them.
In Ramadan no city captures the distinctive aroma of festive food as bewitchingly as Kairouan, especially in the long hours preceding the *iftar,* the evening meal that breaks the month-long period of daylight fasting. Wonderful scents and mouth-watering aromas waft from the doors of homes and bakeries. Driven by these, men run through the market, filling baskets with fresh fruits. Enticed by other scents yet more queue to buy bread fresh from the oven. Each one of them feels blessed when he can open his colourfully woven *kufa* (basket), to add the hot bread. They become greedy and want three or

four varieties of loaf, one of each kind to grace the over-loaded family table. These preparations turn the city into an operatic set, as the seasonal flurry of *burnouses* in winter, or *jebbahs* in summer intensifies, the sun sinks in the western sky, and the world's largest dinner party begins. People are not driven solely by hunger, but by the powerful sense of belonging within the Muslim tent. The community it creates reaches a proud climax and generates a special atmosphere that everyone should witness, with its exotic range of traditional fare and its backdrop of bewitching aromas. If you cannot join the celebrations, then try some of the recipes that follow. Remember that food offers a bridge between the sometimes tense worlds of Islam and Christianity. Many Muslims tuck into Christmas turkeys and Christians are welcomed at *iftar* feasts. Then, once you have ticked this box on your list of lifetime things to do, add a bar mitzvah to your list. They are all joyous occasions, open to guests of any religion.

One woman in history did more than any other to restore the balance between men and women in our city. In Kairouan, perhaps even more than elsewhere, the lady of the house rules the kitchen and takes her responsibilities seriously. In the reign of the first Abbasid Caliph Abu Jaafar Al-Mansour, one clever local fiancée called Arwa, negotiated an unusual marriage contract with him. It brought her lasting fame, because it stipulated that her husband could not take a second wife, while married to her, without her consent. If he did so, Arwa could divorce him. This stipulation became known as the 'Kairouan marriage contract'. When the Caliph recognized the justice of such a proviso her renown was assured. The women of Kairouan inherited her right to file for divorce in these circumstances, a privilege previously limited to men at the time. This right was later preserved by the new republic, and incorporated into Tunisia's remarkable Personal Status Code of 1956. The Kairouan Marriage Contract went national and, as anyone who has read my autobiography will know, I have every reason to be grateful for Arwa's initiative and for this courageous act of reform.

With the rise of the Ottoman Empire Tunisia aligned itself to the Sultan. Some tasteful and well-presented dishes from the Ottoman Palace then appeared on Tunisian tables. They had been collected from all over Muslim Asia. Such rare and exotic dishes inspired the introduction of *mezze* into Asian Arab lands. The Bey of Tunis ruling on behalf of the Turkish Authority then exposed his subjects to a regime that honoured and promoted culinary excellence. As in many Arab lands this Turkish culinary legacy is rich. Today, after eighty years of European settlement under French colonial rule, Turkish coffee and tea, for example, continued to be served in Tunisian cafés, homes and government offices. Other European lands left their calling cards, too. On northern coasts sea-food is handled with almost Spanish devotion, while pasta-eating habits in Sousse follow Italian cuisine. For centuries Tunisians had kept in touch with caravan routes to the east and shipping to the north. By this time the people of Tunisia had acquired the rare skill of assimilating diverse eating habits into their diet.

But the strongest and most influential source of innovation has yet to be described. It presented a more acceptable Muslim style to the whole population. Its influence was not confined to the kitchen. It covered the arts, architecture, music and traditional dress and it crept gradually, almost unnoticed under the radar beam of history. Today Tunisia rightly claims the architecture of Sidi Bou Said, Malouf music, and the *chechia* and other forms of headwear, as jewels in its national heritage. All have been traced by Kairouan-born, Emeritus Professor Abdeljalil Temimi, of the University of Tunis, as exports from Muslim Andalusia. The 1492 exodus of Moors and Jews from Spain eventually resettled many new families in coastal Tunisia, where they prospered. More than a hundred thousand were attracted by the

Kairouan, founded as a military base in AD 670 rivalled the great centres of Basra and Kufa in its heyday. To this day, it remains a pivotal centre of the country's identity, with its Great Mosque **(above)** *very much at its centre.*

welcome on offer to them. This is yet another example of Tunisia's traditional policy of open doors and its hospitable disposition. In 1967 a conversation with the young director of Tunisia's National Theatre, Ali Ben Ayed, rebeefed that, even after five centuries of exile, his family still treasured the front door key to their former home in Granada. Sidi Bou Said is a delightfully situated version of the 'white villages' of Andalusia. Tunisian ceramics in Nabeul can trace their ancestry to Spain and, from there, back to Persia and the Silk Road to China. These links amount to a truly monumental reunion of multiple cultural achievements for humanity to celebrate.

The dinner table which lies at the heart of most celebrations was similarly affected. Couscous recipes are among rare examples of a fusion between cereal, potatoes and tomatoes. Professor Temimi attributes this fusion to later settlers from Andalusia. The potato and tomato were fruits of the discovery of America brought back to Spain by Columbus. He suggests that Moors also brought the new products to Tunisia and used them to enrich their couscous. The Tunisian *tajin*'s similarity to the Spanish tortilla implies a further link. The *rosata* is the *horchata* of Valencia and so on. Taking these factors into account, the assimilation of the Moors into Tunisian society has produced the most distinctive of all the culinary additions it has witnessed in modern times.

Foreword

The music of Tunisia is the product of a mélange of influences ranging as far apart as Andalusia and Turkey, as well as the broader Arab world.

In writing this book I have come to realise how my grandmother familiarized me with many of the culinary traditions that lie buried in Tunisia's past. I remember Omi Rekaya, for that is what we called her, making couscous by hand at home with the help of family and neighbours, to whom she also lent her support. It was she who taught me the importance of healthy eating, and who introduced me to the dishes that comprise the Tunisian art of cookery. She taught me to buy only the freshest vegetables and to check their colour and texture before making a purchase, because cookery was the medium through which she voiced her values. She reflected on how best to prepare meat dishes in particular, because they marked a lamb's final curtain-call on earth. And she thought of the farmer who had raised it, giving it water and fertilizing the field in which it grazed. The neighbour who treated the lamb in her pot, as if the poor beast was made of cardboard upset her. The lives of birds and animals had value, which must be respected when prepared for the table. Care over cookery celebrated their lives. This courtesy also extended to vegetables. If she decided to cook artichokes, she would hold one up to admire, as if it were a work of art, as she looked for inspiration as to the best way to cook it. For this artist at work the kitchen was her studio.

Her thoughts chime with today's vegan dietary trend, but they were present in pre-industrial times, too, and continue to be embraced by many good chefs. She had a rich supply of proverbs about food and its preparation and held firm views on every aspect of cookery, and how best to eat it: 'Eat slowly live long'; or 'A wasteful cook makes an enemy of her household'. Grandmother loved cooking but she always left room for fresh fruit. Her winter table groaned under plates of dates and citrus fruits, which lasted almost until apricots and medlars announced the arrival of summer varieties. 'A season without fruits' she was heard to declare, 'deserves no name', or 'a varied diet cures more than the doctor'. Her concern extended to all aspects of cookery. She experimented with new dishes. Her sayings were the pearls of the domestic philosophy by which she lived. She plucked them from her anthology of ancestral beliefs and injected everything she valued in the kitchen into my young head, initiating me to customs and traditions stretching back to antiquity. If any of them have been misrepresented the error is mine. I deeply appreciate her insights which have served me well.

The Tunisian Republic has protected the ancient strengths of its peoples and built on their culinary traditions, too. The age of science has caught up with the domestic kitchen. Food production and agriculture have been industrialized. International tourism, although currently paused for reasons of global emergency, has professionalized the catering industry and enriched the range of meals presented to our visitors. The buffet service favoured by the hospitality industry has devised, first an impressive range of salads and dishes served at room temperature, followed by new technologies to relocate self service cooking facilities in the dining area of hotels. In this way a distinctive new Tunisian cuisine is emerging from popular domestic traditions. It adds much to the formula that has successfully grown the industry. These changes are no longer confined to hotels. Cafés and saloons specializing in serving cakes, pizzas, ice-creams and a growing range of snacks and soft drinks have also appeared in the coastal tourist hotspots. Among them coca cola and hamburgers are also available. The *casse-croute* of the early years of the Republic was a nutritious sandwich roll, filled with pickled vegetables fresh tomato and a generous daub of *harissa*. In this generation it has turned into the beginnings of a street food bonanza. One street food style recipe for fricassee is included. It may turn out to be a major step towards a new style of eating. In the meantime, it deserves mention as an indicator of how Tunisian cooking skills remain open to change and keep pace with our need to travel in hope towards a future filled with new opportunities.

Now join me on a journey through aromas, tastes and colours. Prepare to pamper your senses. They, too, will enjoy the spicy, sun-drenched holiday that lies within this book. Tunis lies closer to London than Athens, and yet it feels exotically both African and Oriental. After the section on spices and condiments comes an array of preserves to help enhance the tastes of this cuisine. Cereals in turn follow because they have an important place in the Tunisian cuisine, alas, only a short list is included. Do not be overwhelmed to find 'Special recipes for celebrations' heading the groups of recipe on offer. Some, but not all, are challenging. Their presence is a monument to their significance for the people of Tunisia, who celebrate them through the memories they stimulate. You may want to try some. But, if you would rather stick to what you sampled in restaurants or on holiday, feel free to do so. A variety of couscous recipes are included although they are not the only Tunisian dishes with universal appeal. *Briks* and *tajin*s are well worth exploring, too. Cakes and puddings are also mouth-watering. Some need careful presentation, but filo pastry can now be made more easily in a domestic setting. You may be able to surprise yourself. Your journey may begin on the pages of a book, but it will involve shopping for the ingredients, cooking and sampling, and sharing this adventure with your nearest and dearest. I suggest that you start with some of the more straightforward dishes. *Tajin* recipe (p. 68), whole chicken soup (p. 78), grilled salad (p. 102), and carrot salad (p. 109), are ideal candidates. In a cook's mindset experiment and change are essential

tools. A thoughtful tweak may help you to adapt them to your taste and circumstances. Then you may begin to share my conviction that the best of Tunisian cuisine merits fuller representation on the world stage.

The book stretches into a past, which may remind my compatriots of their nation's rich history and times when women could spend time together, exchanging secrets from each others' larders. One book '*Les Lettres de Noblesse de la Gastronomie Tunisienne*' 2019, by Jacob Lelouch, explores the contributions of accommodating recipes from the three religious communities and their different calendars of feast days. This book confirms shared traditions of hospitality and culinary roots stretching back to the very beginnings of history.

My belief is that every country that honours its past also works hard to secure its future. At the time of writing, one learned doctor has bridged the gap that has, until today, existed between the art of cookery and

The village of Sidi Bou Said, **(above)**, *named after a religious figure who lived there, has become an iconic representation of the Mediterranean idyll. The so-called 'white villages' follow a very distinctive style and can be found across Tunisia and as far away as southern Spain.*

the science of nutrition. Dr. Simon Poole's *The real Mediterranean diet – A practical guide to understanding and achieving the healthiest diet in the world* offers genuine messages of hope for all of us. He comes close to convincing that there exists a true boundary separating advertising propaganda from science, reminds all of the need for fruit and vegetables to be fresh and seasonal, and guides his readers towards and along a credibly detailed pathway to healthier eating. Why is he more credible than a number of other writers? Because he accounts for several of the unexplained social problems of our age. He explains why dieting fails to deliver lasting results and why obesity spreads rapidly across the industrialized world in particular. And he does not claim that science yet has all the answers - there is much more to learn through further investigation. His advice to reduce consumption of manufactured foodstuffs and return to kitchen produced meals is a wholesome truth to be heeded. His motivation in writing a book on Mediterranean cuisine adds voice to the convictions set out in this book. In summary Tunisia has adopted selected innovations over the centuries from cuisines all around the Mediterranean Sea and has adapted them to the domestic environment of its homes and farms.

If this is correct then Tunisian cooks will continue to delight their customers for many years to come. It is also my sincere hope that you will enjoy sharing in this culinary adventure as much as I have enjoyed researching, cooking and writing up. *Shahia Taiba* is the Arabic phrase to wish you a hearty appetite for an interestingly liberating journey! But please remember that all this has been achieved through the skills and determination of Tunisian mothers who have passed their culinary culture down the generations.

A NOTE ON INGREDIENTS

Preserved Cereals
Traditionally couscous was hand-made by every home-maker with help from family members, friends and neighbours. The favour was returned and women spent weeks in the August season, going from one home to another to lend a hand. This important social event guarded against malnutrition by providing wholesome food for families to eat.

Today almost all couscous is shop bought. Only traditional families still commission it from a few surviving artisans. Within living memory women still diversified the family diet by making *mhamas*, *borghol*, *malthouth*, *hlelem*, *rechta* and *chorba frik*, from a couscous base, but in varied shapes. Prepared in a basically similar way they looked and tasted different. Some were made from barley. They are mentioned as a reminder of diverse culinary traditions. Some survive on the commercial market, others only thanks to a few champions.

Yet more home-prepared ingredients e.g. dried okra, tomato paste, dried tomato, preserved green and black olives, capers, gherkins, chilli or lemon in brine, various salted vegetables and grilled salads are still prepared by senior members of the family for domestic use. My fervent hope is that some will thrive commercially, while others will be kept alive by other means. In a vote for their survival, recipes using cracked wheat (*borghol*) and *hlelem* are found among the soups.

The range of couscous dishes using different meats – fish, dried meat, merguez (spicy lamb sausages), chicken, fish, seafood, or rabbit – extends far beyond the few listed here and could easily fill the book. I offer humble apologies for overlooking everyone's favourite family recipe and beg them, please, to send it instead to family members studying abroad and English-speaking friends.

Preserved meats
In the days before domestic refrigeration many techniques for preserving meat and fish were used. For those interested in our history here are two:-

1 - Preserved meat was cut in thin slices, well rubbed with powdered black pepper and salt and put outside in the sun to dry. Sheep's tail fat was then melted in a sealable jar and the dried pieces of meat added. The container was then sealed and stored in the larder. The meat remained fresh-tasting for months.

2 - Dried octopus is still sold in the coastal towns of the Sahel and Sfax, and used to season *chakchouka*s, sauces and soups.

The following standard abbreviations are used through this book:-
pounds (lbs), ounces (oz), tablespoons (tbsps), teaspoons (tsps), kilos (kg), grams (g), temperature (100°C), centimetre/s (cm/s), minute/s (mn/s)
Cups refer to standard US cup measurements

THE A TO Z OF TUNISIAN SPICES

Tunisian cooks keep many of the following spices in their store:-

1. Aniseed (powdered), is used in home-made bread and cakes made with sorghum.
2. Black pepper. No kitchen can do without it.
3. Bay leaf is used for tomato dishes and certain stews like *molokhiyeh*.
4. Caraway seeds are used to season vegetable dishes like *omok houria*.
5. Cayenne Pepper is made from hot peppers and is widely used to give dishes a lift.
6. Cinnamon is used in powder form, in cakes like *makroudh*, or mixed with other spices, as in *ras il hanout*. It is used to season wild game and some stews like *bnadaqs*. Stick cinnamon is used in some puddings.
7. Cloves are used sparingly, mainly in *ras il hanout*.
8. Coriander is seldom used alone in powder form, but in combination with other spices to season *bsisa*, or mixed with cumin in some stews. Its leaf seasons vegetable dishes.
9. Cumin powder is used for certain soups, *chakchouka* and sauces for fish.
10. Dill is used in vegetable dishes and is often complemented by coriander leaves.
11. Garlic is widely used in soups, *chakchoukas*, stews and tomato sauces to accompany most types of meats and pasta.
12. Geranium essence, rose water and orange blossom, add flavour and fragrance to puddings and cakes.
13. Ginger is dried and ground and used to flavour *sohleb*.
14. *Harissa* comes in different varieties, all of which contain hot chillies, peeled and made into a puree.
15. *Hrous* is a mix of spices used in the South of Tunisia, made from onions or hot chillis pulped and seasoned with coriander, caraway seeds and rose petals. In summer an annual household supply is prepared for use in many dishes.
16. Lemons are extensively used in soups and vinaigrettes, *briks*, savoury fritters, stews and fish dishes. And in refreshing lemonades.
17. Mint leaves are dried and used to flavour mint tea, a national specialty. They are also used powdered in *chakchouka*s, soups, *qadid*, *merguez* and sparingly in fresh salads.
18. Olive oil. Every Tunisian larder has it in store.
19. Orange peel is dried and cut in cubes. It is used to flavour stews like *molokhiyeh*. Its powder flavours cakes like baklava
20. Paprika adds colour to many dishes.
21. Saffron is popular for adding colour and aroma to stews, roast meats, chicken and fish. It is never used with *harissa*, chili pepper, coriander or caraway.
22. Sage is used for tomato dishes and certain stews like *molokhiyeh*.
23. *Tabil* is a mix of dried and ground spices (coriander, caraway, garlic and cayenne pepper), and used in stews, vegetable dishes and most beef and beef dishes.
24. Tomato paste is widely used in sauces to accompany fish, stews, couscous, pasta dishes and vegetables. Formerly made in an annual supply, it is now shop bought.
25. Vinegar is used to pickle and preserve capers, gherkins, small onions or carrots and sometimes replaces lemon juice, in vinaigrettes. It is usually distilled white vinegar.

HEALTHY CUISINE

Making Essences
Essences make an important contribution to Tunisian dishes. In my youth April was the moment when rose petals, geranium leaves, jasmine flowers and orange blossom were sold in the market and the domestic distilling season lasted the whole month. Women visited each other's homes to lend a helping hand in the same way as for couscous. Kairouan was famed for perfume-making. For a season fragrances filled the air. In every house a cauldron of water was put to heat, with an alembic still filled with petals perched on top. From its spout essence fell, drop by drop into waiting bottles. This activity lasted for four to five days and would meet the family's needs for the entire year. The essences were used as a toiletry, as an aid to digestion and as flavouring for cakes and puddings. You will find a number of recipes using these essences. If not sold locally they can be ordered on-line. They helped to keep people cool and fragrant through the summer heat.

The health benefits of ingredients used in Tunisian cuisine
The Tunisian diet is notably healthy. Some of its traditional staples are among the richest sources of food essentials – dried apricots contain more fibre than prunes, and the chickpea is the pulse richest in proteins. Both are also good to eat. Several superfoods, most notably olive oil, have long been prominent in our diet:

- **Tomatoes**: A major dietary source of the antioxidant lycopene (a natural cancer fighter) and are linked to other health benefits, including protection from heart disease. They are also a source of vitamins C, A, and K and potassium. Their anti-inflammatory properties may also help reduce high blood pressure and protect against blood clots. For men, according to *Food as Medicine*, they guard against prostate problems. They are eaten every day by most Tunisians.
- **Garlic**: According to *Food as Medicine* it protects from colds and lowers cholesterol.
- **Olive oil**: This oil is rich in mono-unsaturated fats, is rich in antioxidants and has strong anti-inflammatory properties. It protects against heart disease. New research shows that a half tablespoon a day in one's diet leads to improved cardiovascular health and lower blood pressure.
- **Peppers**: Claim to have medicinal effects similar to those found in cough syrups, but caution is recommended, because too much hot chili pepper can irritate the stomach.
- **Lemons**: Are a good source of vitamin C and help control weight. They prevent kidney stones, protect against anaemia and improve digestive health.
- **Onions**: They, too contain antioxidants, compounds that fight inflammation and reduce cholesterol levels – all of which may lower heart disease risk. They help ease constriction of bronchial tubes which is beneficial for asthma sufferers.
- **Harissa**: Is made out of chili peppers which are said to contain chemicals that boost fat burning, and help curb appetite, and thereby weight loss.
- **Couscous**: See section on couscous.
- **Fish**: Contains nutrients that are crucial to growing children. It is said to feed the brain health, prevent and treat depression. It is a good dietary source of vitamin D and helps reduce risk of auto-immune diseases. For children it is said to prevent asthma. 'Food as Medicine'

claims that it prevents headaches and is beneficial for arthritis sufferers.

- **Chickpeas:** The most environmentally friendly legume, recognised as a superfood by the United Nations, as well as governments and food agencies around the world. An ideal food for protein and fibre, which also protects the planet
- **Tea:** Green tea is the most frequently used Tunisian drink. Regular doses of tea reduce the risk of stroke. 'Food as Medicine' tells us that tea suppresses appetite and keeps the immune system healthy.
- **Dates:** Rich in natural sugars and fibre, many claims are made on behalf of their antioxidant and anti-inflammatory characteristics. They are also rich in vitamins B1, B2, B3, and B5.

The above ingredients are important to the Tunisian diet. Other regular parts of the diet have also been described as superfoods offering multiple benefits. They include: olive oil, spinach, watermelon and parsley, which benefit skin, hair and bones. Others, like carrots, cucumbers and pumpkin, are high in fibre which aids digestion. Example of nuts and fruits with claimed benefits are:-

- **Almonds:** Packed full of protein and natural fats, they are better eaten with the skin on them. Almond oil also strengthens finger and toenails when directly applied.
- **Apples:** They are eaten as a fresh fruit, added to salads and made into cakes and puddings. Each apple has 4 grams of fibre and is packed with nutrients, vitamin B, and antioxidants to ward off diseases.
- **Oranges:** Are a daily dose of sunshine. According to 'Food as Medicine' they lower cholesterol, prevent and dissolve kidney stones and reduce the risk of colon cancer.
- **Pears:** Contain vitamin C, A and D, and are a rich source of fibre which assists digestion, lower levels of cholesterol and help weight loss.
- **Pomegranates:** a goddess among fruits, they are a super food whose benefits range from antioxidants to the claimed prevention of certain cancers. That is why a Tunisian song celebrates them.
- **Watermelon:** 'Food as Medicine' calls it the coolest thirst quencher. It has a 92% water content. It contains glutathione which helps boost our immune system, and lycopene, a cancer fighting oxidant. Other nutrients found in watermelon are vitamin C & potassium.

Measurements, weights & temperature
All recipes are for four adults unless specifically stated otherwise. Weights and measures used are given both in metric and U.S. units. Temperature is measured in centigrade. For eggs, standard medium size is used. Although important to all cooking, the quantities of salt and pepper used are left to individual taste. If *harissa* is new to you, you will want to experiment with it. The book uses Tunisian quantities, which may be excessive for your taste. Use less. You can always add more, if you want.
For temperature Celsius is used. Here are equivalents in Fahrenheit.

Very hot:	240 = 450
Hot:	200 = 400
Moderate hot:	190 = 375
Moderate/medium:	175 = 350
Medium-low heat:	140/160 =300/400
Warm:	165 = 325
Slow/low:	150 = 300
Simmer:	90 = 200

Heating can be done on a hob or an oven. If you have an electric stove with nine-step knobs, medium-low heat, for example is 3-4 which equates to 140°C to 160°C (= 300° F to 400°F). If you have six-step knobs on your electric stoves, 2-3 is the medium-low heat. This is the general temperature for food to be cooked thoroughly, if not instructed otherwise.

Dishes for Special Occasions

P. 36 **Shorbat Frik**

P. 39 **Kairouan Makroudh**

P. 41 **Mrayish**

P. 42 **The Bey's Baklava**

P. 44 **Zlebia**

Dishes for Special Occasions

'New dishes beget new appetites.'

The Tunisian calendar follows the lunar year and is punctuated by festivities. Each one carries a distinctive religious significance and is accompanied by its own special recipes. There are three Eids (festivals) in each year: Eid Milad En Nabi (the birthday of the Prophet Mohamed), Eid Al-Fitr and Eid Al-Adha. For these festivities particular dishes are dedicated to the occasion. At the conclusion of Ramadan *zakat* (a levy on the fasting person) is offered as a token of thanks to God for the discipline that helped people to observe the obligatory month-long daylight fast and, of course, to share their feast with their less fortunate co-religionists.

Eid Milad En Nabi is the festival commemorating the birth of the Prophet Mohammed. It is believed that he was born in Mecca in 570 CE, and it is in many ways the Islamic equivalent to Christmas. The day starts with morning prayers followed by a procession and large gatherings in mosques. Children are told stories of the Prophet and his life. The day ends with donations to those in need.

Eid Al-Fitr (or the Feast of Breaking the Fast) marks the end of Ramadan. It brings happiness and rejoicing and as such is celebrated not just with new clothes, but also with visits to family and friends to eat sweets, drink coffee and celebrate.

Eid Al-Adha (or Feast of the Sacrifice) honours the readiness of the Patriarch Abraham to sacrifice his son as an act of obedience. Before Abraham could follow through and sacrifice his son, however, God provided a lamb to sacrifice instead. In memory of this today, one

third of a lamb's meat is consumed by the family, a second third is given to the poor and the last third is made into *qadid* – dried meat for later. Sweets and gifts are given, and family visits are hospitably exchanged. The purpose of Ramadan is to teach the practices of self-discipline, self-control, sacrifice and empathy for the less fortunate, by encouraging acts of generosity and charity.

A hybrid of couscous is served at every special occasion. In the holy month of Ramadan a couscous dessert is prepared with milk and a little honey for the sundown *iftar*, when the day's fasting has ended. It is called *masfouf*. In Eid Milad en Nabi a dessert from honey, *smen* (a type of fermented butter) and semolina is prepared, along with baklava and rice pudding. *Tharida* is often also prepared – a soup dish made from broth, stewed meat and breadcrumbs. For Eid Al-Fitr, *kaak*, a bagel-shaped biscuit stuffed with dates, is also prepared. Sweets, treats and local delicacies such as Turkish *halwa*, fruit cakes, dates stuffed with almonds and dried fruits almonds and pistachios are all part of the festive spirit of these occasions. At the end of the Islamic *hijri* year extra chickpeas and dried meats (*qadid*), are added to the normal recipes.

For the Eid Al Adha celebration couscous with *osban* is served. The arrival of Spring is celebrated with lamb couscous garnished with added dried fruits. Couscous remains the Tunisian dish of choice for celebrations. It is frequently served at family events, such as weddings, births and circumcisions. It celebrates plentiful times.

Dishes for Special Occasions

Shorbat Frik

Serves 4
Cooking time: 1h 40mins

500g / 1 lb 2 oz meat or chicken cut into small pieces
62g / ½ cup *frik* (green wheat)
1 small onion chopped
2 tbsps chopped celery
2 tbsps coriander leaves
2 tbsps chickpeas
85g / ¾ cup canned tomato purée
2 tbsp olive oil
3 cloves garlic crushed
1 tbsp *ras el hanout* crushed
1 tsp paprika
2 pinches cayenne pepper
½ tsp dry mint
Salt and pepper to taste

This dish appears on Tunisian dinner tables on almost all twenty-nine nights of Ramadan. It is especially well loved in the fasting month because its hearty ingredients of meat, *frik* and stock both quench thirst and satisfy hunger.

Mix crushed garlic and crushed *ras el hanout*. In a large pot put the oil to heat on medium heat. Add the garlic and *ras el hanout*, the chopped onion, paprika, cayenne pepper, salt, pepper and the tomato sauce and gently fry for 3-4 minutes until the spices release their fragrance.

Add the meat or chicken pieces and continue to fry gently. If needed a little water may be added to stop the meat from sticking to the bottom. When the meat or chicken is golden, add chickpeas and enough water for your soup – about a couple of litres should be right. You can always add more later on in the cooking process.

Add the *frik* or green wheat and celery and lower the heat to simmer for about 50 to 60 minutes. Check and taste the cooking 30 minutes after the start – you may need to add water or seasoning.

When almost ready, add coriander leaves and dried mint. Serve hot with your favourite fresh bread.

Kairouan Makroudh

Serves 4
Cooking time: 1h 10mins
(Dough standing: 3h)

For the dough:
500g (4 cups) semolina
125g (1 cup) flour
125g (1 cup) *smen* (clarified butter)
¾ of a tsp baking powder
2 pinches (½ tsp) salt
30g (4 tbsps) orange blossom water
125ml (½ cup) warm water
1 litre (about 4 cups) vegetable oil (the *makroudh* is deep fried)

For the date filling:
300g (2½ cups) dates with stones removed
2 tbsps *smen* (clarified butter)
3 tbsps (1½ oz) orange blossom water
½ tbsp ground cinnamon
½ tsp ground cloves

...cont'd next page

No special occasion in Kairouan is complete without *makroudh*. For the sugar-loving Kairouanese, it is not just the city's signature dish but its very identity. People travel great distances to buy the best *makroudh* – from all over Tunisia but also as far afield as neighbouring Algeria and Libya. The delicacy is prominently displayed in every patisserie, served to family and friends and offered proudly to foreigners.

Its name is derived from is unusual diamond shape. Traditionally in order to warrant the name of *makroudh*, Kairouanese makers must use an olive wood mould with a relief design featuring the mausoleum of the local saint. Things of course have changed a bit, but it is still said that its distinctive form brings together wheat from the earth, dates from the tree, honey from the bee and skill from the hands that make it. It is hailed as a marriage of a baker's skills allied with natural ingredients, all working in harmony to produce the best possible mouthful of flavour.

As such, *makroudh* is in many ways the key to unlock Kairouan's happy memories, as testified by the annual Makroudh Festival which has been held in the city since 2008.

When I was a little girl there was only one kind of *makroudh*, made with dates. In recent years a new generation of cake makers have added variety. Instead of dates, experiments with almonds, pistachios, walnuts and figs have found success in the market. Even white *makroudh*, made without its colourful injection of turmeric, has attracted a following. But for the purist, the original date-filled *makroudh* remains the best-selling choice and the classic recipe, given below, vividly recalls my childhood.

1.

Kairouan Makroudh

For the syrup:
A generous ½ cup (4 oz) of honey
2 tbsps (1 oz) of orange blossom water
Juice of 1 lemon

1. Blend the dates and mix them well with the butter, orange blossom water, cinnamon and cloves until you obtain a smooth paste. Set aside.
2. In a large bowl pour the semolina, the flour and the baking powder and mix well. Make a well where you pour the melted butter. Work in the mixture of semolina and flour a bit at a time until obtaining a smooth dough. Leave to stand for three hours. Sprinkle over the orange blossom water and the warm water and with your fingertips work the dough and knead it well. If the dough is too hard add a little water to soften it. The resulting dough needs to be compact before you can cover it with cling film. Then leave to stand for one hour.
3. Take a handful of dough and shape it into a sausage. With the index finger make a canal lengthwise in the centre. Take a little bit of the date paste and roll it into a slimmer sausage. Place it in the canal and pull the edges of the dough back over the date paste to cover it. Roll the whole thing once more to get a sausage-like shape of about 2.5cms (1 inch) diameter. Cut diamond shapes which you place on a baking sheet. Repeat until all the dough is used.
4. Heat a large pot with oil and deep fry the *makroudh* on each side until brown. Make sure to arrange the diamonds close to each other so that the dates do not burn. When ready place them on a paper sheet so that the oil is absorbed.
5. Over low heat (150°C / 300°F) cook the honey, orange blossom water and the lemon juice for 20-25 minutes. Away from the heat, and while the *makroudh* is still warm, dip both sides of the cake in the mixture. Set aside for an hour before serving.

Note: *Makroudh* keeps for a few weeks when kept in an airtight box.

Mrayish

Serves 4
Cooking time: 1h 10mins

Beja Chicken with Pistachios. This scrumptious dish is cooked for newly-weds on the day after their wedding. It is also served at the final lunch before Ramadan.

500g semolina
1 whole medium chicken (1kg / 2.2 lbs)
1 pint milk
100g (1 cup) pistachios
100g (1 cup) almonds
100g (1 cup) raisins
6 tbsp (¾ cup) olive oil
Salt and black pepper to taste

Thoroughly clean the chicken. Cut it into pieces, season with salt and black pepper. Heat only half a cup of the oil and fry the pieces until golden.

Cover with water, bring to the boil and lower the heat to simmer for 45 minutes.

At the same time blanch the almonds and gently grill them with the shelled pistachios.

Knead the semolina with the remaining quarter cup of olive oil, salt to taste and sprinkle with enough warm water to keep the dough easy to handle. Leave to rest for an hour and make thin pancakes. In a pre-heated oven marked 180°C put them to cook for 10 to 15 minutes. Take the pancakes out and crumble them. Check seasoning when the chicken is cooked.

Boil the fresh milk. Drizzle it with the broth made from the chicken, onto the crumbled pancakes. Decorate with the dried fruits and the chicken pieces.

Serve hot.

The Bey's Baklava

Serves 4
Cooking time: 15 mins

10 filo pastry rounds (Purchase is recommended where possible)
185g (1½ cups) unsalted butter
125g (1 cup) ground almonds
125g (1 cup) ground hazelnuts
125g (1 cup) ground walnuts
125g (1 cup) ground pistachios
125g (1 cup) caster sugar
60g (½ cup) rose water
1 lemon for juice
1 tsp cinnamon
125g (1 cup) clear honey

My aunt Fatma's recipe. No special occasion passes without this special dish. It is also my husband's favourite cake and (see my autobiography) the sweet that President Bourguiba encouraged me to sample. He told me it was his favourite, too. Aunt Fatma was an excellent cook and patissier and had a thriving business catering for weddings and special occasions.

Butter a 25cm (10 inches) square baking tin. Heat the 1½ cups of unsalted butter. Stack two filo pastry sheets at a time making sure they fill the baking tray. Spray thoroughly with the melted butter. Pour the ground almonds on top of the filo pastry and level out this layer.

Baste a mixture of one tablespoon of rose water, one teaspoon of lemon juice and one tablespoon of caster sugar and drizzle over the pastry. Repeat the same procedure with the next two filo pastry sheets but adding hazelnuts instead of almonds. Again repeat the same procedure with another two filo pastry layers, adding hazelnuts and pistachios in turn. Cover with the last two filo pastry sheets. Finally baste with the rest of the melted butter, a tablespoon of caster sugar, one teaspoon of lemon juice and a sprinkle of cinnamon.

Put in a hot oven pre-heated to 200°C, and cook for 10-15 minutes or until the filo pastry is crisp. Take out of the oven and cut while still hot with a sharp knife into diamond shapes of 3cms (1¼ inches) long.

Heat the honey and baste the top along the cuts. Leave to cool before serving.

Zlebia

Serves 4
Cooking time: 1h

For the dough:
125g (1 cup) flour 380ml (1½ cup) of water
125g (1 cup) cornflour
2 tsps baking powder
2 pinches (½ tsp) cardamom
2 tsps yeast
½ tsp salt
2 pinches (½ tsp) saffron
500ml (2 cups) vegetable oil (or more as needed)

For the syrup:
250g (2 cups) sugar
250ml (1 cup) water or a little more
2 tbsps lemon juice
2 tbsps honey
2 tbsps rose water

This traditional sweet was adopted by the city of Beja, in north-western Tunisia, but is originally from Turkey. It has since spread across the nation for use on special occasions. It is a delicious light fritter dipped in sugar syrup. The distinctive flat circle is obtained by rolling a long thin spiral of dough into a Catherine-wheel shape before plunging it into boiling oil.

Mix yeast, sugar and water. Cover and leave to rest for 20 minutes.

Mix in the cornflour, salt and baking powder. Cover and place in a warm place for 1 hour 15 minutes. The result is a batter and it should be as for a stiff pancake mix. If too thick, add more water until a loose enough consistency is obtained.

Heat the oil to a high temperature. Place the batter in a pastry bag with small tip to shape the *zlebia*. Start from the middle of a spiral. Squeeze the pastry bag and circle outwards to form a flat spiral of about 7cms (2¾ inches) diameter. Then fry the *zlebia*s on both sides. Drain on paper towels. While still warm, dip the *zlebia* in the syrup and allow the excess to drip off.

Tip: Your pan should deep fry the *zlebia* so it floats. If it touches the bottom, it will come out flat and will not rise.

Couscous

P. 50 **Fish Couscous**

P.52 **Chicken Couscous**

P.53 **Lamb Couscous**

Couscous

May good digestion reward a hearty appetite!

The popularity of couscous as an alternative to rice and potatoes in the global diet just grows and grows. One cup of cooked couscous has fewer calories and carbohydrates than equivalent amounts of rice, although brown rice wins when it comes to fibre. Couscous is low in fat and is a slow-release carbohydrate, which means that it takes longer to convert to energy in the body, and keeps it satisfied for longer. Vegetable couscous is also nutritiously vegan-friendly. The accompanying vegetables, tomatoes, carrots, pumpkin, onions, chickpeas, beans and, of course, olive oil are all healthy, low-cost foods, regularly available in western supermarkets. These qualities may help to explain its growing popularity.

When cooked in water instead of steam, the wheat-based semolina is conveniently ready in 5-10 minutes. If the semolina is being prepared in water, using equal amounts of salted water and grains, with, optionally, a few added drops of olive oil and half a stock cube to match the dish you are preparing. It is not strictly necessary to use the couscous pot favoured in couscous homelands.

The couscous pot comes in two parts: a colander called a *keskes* for steaming the semolina, designed to fit tightly over the cooking pot *nhassa*, to allow vapour from it to cook the semolina above. The semolina is sprinkled with water and placed in the *keskes*, and the sauce, vegetables and meats are cooked below in the *nhassa*.

It is from the word *keskes* that couscous gets its name.

Easy way to cook couscous
When cooked in water instead of steam

Couscous

Fish Couscous

Serves 4
Cooking time: 40 mins

My friend Janet's recipe. This South of Tunisia couscous, a recipe from my friend Janet is delicious and very light. You can use mullet, sea bream or grouper, depending on availability in the market.

500g grouper or 750g sea bream or 1kg mullet = 1.1lbs or 1.65lbs or 2.2lbs
500g couscous (4 cups / 1.1lbs)
150g onion (1⅓ cups)
150g potatoes (1⅓ cups)
1 courgette (150g 1⅓ cups
300g cabbage = 2⅓ cups
100g chickpeas = ⅔ cup
1½ litres of water = 6⅓ cups
4g *harissa* = 1½ tbsp
15g tomato purée = 2 tbsp
4g paprika = ½ tbsp
4g cumin = ½ tbsp
30ml olive oil = 2 tbsp
8ml salted butter = ½ tbsp
Salt and pepper to taste

Clean the fish. Season and cut it in large enough pieces so that it will not disintegrate while cooking.
Peel and chop the onion. Heat the oil and the butter. Fry the chopped onion until golden, add the tomato purée, the paprika, the *harissa*, (already diluted in a ½ tablespoon of water), the potatoes peeled and cut in two and the chickpeas already washed. Add the water. Once it starts boiling, reduce to moderate heat and leave to cook gently for 20-25 minutes.

Sprinkle water on the couscous to moisturise and put it in a steamer to cook on top of the broth pot. Alternatively just follow packaging instructions. When ready put the couscous in a large serving dish and ladle the broth generously over it, season and cover for 2-3 minutes so that the couscous absorbs the liquid. Then arrange the fish and vegetables on top of it and serve hot straight away. Put the rest of the broth in a sauce boat so that there is extra sauce for those who want more.

This dish is complete in itself and no starter is needed.

Chicken Couscous

Serves 4
Cooking time: 1h 15 mins

1 small chicken (1 kg) = 2.2 lbs
500g couscous = 4 cups
150g carrots peeled and cut roughly (2 x 3 cm / ¾ x 1¼ inches) = ⅓ cup
150g young turnips peeled and cut (2 x 3 cm / ¾ x 1¼ inches) = ⅓ cup
150g onion peeled and diced (1½ cm / ½ inch) = ⅓ cup
100g of chickpeas from a bottle = ⅔ cup
15g tomato paste = 2 tbsp
200g chopped tomatoes = 1½ cups
150g courgette cut same size as carrots = ⅓ cup
150g aubergine cut as above = ⅓ cup
300g butternut squash (6 by 8cm / 2.3' x 3.1') = 2½ cups
150g green pepper seeded and cut up in 8 pieces = ⅓ cup
45ml olive oil = 3 tbsp
4g *harissa* = ½ tbsp
8g of cinnamon = 1 tbsp
8g cumin = 1 tbsp
8g coriander = 1 tbsp
2 pinches saffron diluted in a bit of water = ½ tsp
Salt and pepper to taste

My recipe. Traditionally a two-part couscous pot is used.

Clean and cut the chicken into 8 pieces (overflow into two pots if easier). Season the pieces with salt, pepper, cumin, coriander and cinnamon. In the bottom pot heat the oil and put the chopped onion to fry (do not let it brown). When translucent add the chicken, seal it and add the tomato paste. Fry for 5-10 minutes longer then add the chopped tomatoes as well as a little salt and pepper. Add the cleaned and drained chickpeas and the *harissa*. Cover with water. Let this simmer for 10-15 minutes. In the meantime peel and cut the carrots and the turnip and add them to the broth. Place the top part of the couscous pot on top and moisten the couscous with a few tablespoons of sprinkled water. Make sure the grains do not stick together. Cover and let cook for 10-15 more minutes.

Put the couscous in a large dish and moisten again with a little more water, Always be careful to ensure that the grains do not stick together. or you could end having a paste rather than couscous. In the bottom pot add the cut up courgette, aubergine, butternut squash and the saffron. Return the couscous over the bottom pot so that it continues cooking over the steam. Cook for another 15 minutes on moderate medium heat. Add the green pepper to the broth and check the seasoning and that the broth is not too dry and has enough water. Let it cook for 5-7 minutes, being careful not to overcook the vegetables.

Pour the couscous into a large dish, drizzle a tablespoon of olive oil season with salt and pepper and pour some of the broth over it. Mix gently so that the couscous absorbs the liquid. The pieces of chicken now go decoratively on top, along with the butternut squash all around and the chickpeas in the middle. Serve the vegetables in another large bowl and the broth in a sauce boat. You may want to serve separately a little *harissa* in a tiny dish for those who like it hot. Serve hot. *Bon appétit!*

Lamb Couscous

Serves 4
Cooking time: 1h 20 mins

600g leg of lamb cut in 8 pieces = 5 cups = 1.3lbs
60g lamb fat (by tradition the tail but any part of the fat will do) cut in 2 pieces = ½ cup = 2.3oz
600g couscous = 5 cups
150g onion peeled and chopped in squares = 1 ¼ cups
150g medium potatoes peeled and halved = 1 ¼ cups
150g carrots peeled and cut in 7/8 cm long and 2 cm wide = 1¼ cups
150g turnips peeled and cut in 3cm squares = 1 ¼ cups
65g stick of celery cut up crudely = ½ cup
100g chickpeas = ¾ cup
15g tomato purée = 2 tbsp
15g *harissa* (or less to taste) = 2 tbsp
1 tsp cinnamon
1 tsp dried rose buds which have been ground
1 tsp cinnamon
2 tsps paprika
45ml olive oil = 3 tbsp
4g salted butter = 1½ tbsp
4 pints of water
Salt and pepper to taste

Put the lamb in the lower sector of the couscous pot. Season it with salt, pepper, paprika and *harissa*. Add the olive oil and the onions thickly cut. Fry for a little while until the onions became translucent and the meat loses its bloody look. Add a glass of water and the tomato purée. Drain and wash. and the chickpeas and add in. Leave to cook on medium heat for 15-20 minutes. Add the vegetables (carrots, turnips, potatoes and celery). Pour in 1.5 litres of water and bring to the boil.

Sprinkle a handful of water over the couscous and put it in the upper part of the couscous pot, making sure the grains are not stuck together. Cook on moderate medium heat 175°C for 30-40 minutes from the moment the steam starts rising to the upper part of the couscous pot. Then pour it into a large bowl, moisten it once more with a handful of water, working it all the while to liberate the grains of couscous so that they do not stick together. Put it back in the upper part of the couscous pot (for a second cooking) over the lower part, and carry on cooking for another 20 minutes. Pour the couscous into a large serving dish. Skim the fat from the broth. Throw in the lamb tail fat. Add the butter and the spices. Sprinkle the sauce over the couscous. Check the seasoning. Decorate with the cooked lamb and the vegetables. Serve hot.

Vegetable couscous: This recipe, excluding meat, chicken or fish, makes an excellent vegetable couscous. Vegetarians need only add extra chickpeas and beans for a better protein mix.

Briks - Savoury Pies

P. 59 **Egg Briks**

P.60 **Chicken Briks**

P.61 **Vegetables Cakes**

Briks
Savoury Pies

May good digestion reward a hearty appetite!

Brik is a Tunisian curiosity of Ottoman origin. Just like couscous, *brik* creates a special atmosphere around the meal table. It is a truly national dish and one of which we are all very proud and is definitely a Tunisian signature dish. It is eaten at almost every *Iftar* in the month of Ramadan.

This delicate deep-fried envelope of pastry is usually filled with a satisfying slurp of egg skilfully rendered so that the white is cooked and the yolk is runny. It is something that can make overseas visitors wary, but it is fun to eat. The puff pastry that makes the *brik* is called *malsuqa*. In the past Tunisians made *malsuqa* at home. It is a paper thin, transparent pastry, so thin in fact that it is thinner than any pastry on sale in Europe. Nowadays it is available in Tunisian supermarkets, as thin as the traditional homemade pastry.

Briks are typically triangular-shaped, larger than Indian samosas. They are deep fried and therefore risk becoming a bit greasy, but this is counteracted by the lemons which are an essential accompaniment.

Egg Briks

Serves 4
Cooking time: 20 mins

4 eggs
1 onion (125g) = 1 cup
10g parsley = 1½ tbsp
1 lemon
4 *malsuqa* (puff pastry) sheets 25cm diameter
½ cup olive oil
Salt and black pepper to taste

Samah Ben Rejeb's recipe

Cook the peeled onion and the cleaned parsley in a little salted water. Strain it, mash it and season with salt and black pepper. Heat the oil to 200° C. On a plate spread the *malsuqa* puff pastry. Place a little of the stuffing in the middle and make an egg-sized hole in it. Then break a raw egg into the middle of the stuffing. Gently fold the puff pastry in half. Put the plate over the frying pan and slide the *brik* into the hot oil to deep-fry it. Turn it once to brown the other side. Dry on a paper towel.

Make sure you fry separately, one *brik* at a time.

Serve hot with slices of lemon.

Chicken Briks

Serves 4
Cooking time: 30 mins

200g chicken breast = 1¾ cups
4 eggs
200g potatoes = 1¾ cups
1 onion (125g) = 1 cup
50g parsley = ¾ cup
1 lemon
Salt and black pepper to taste
8 *malsuqa* puff pastry sheets
½ cup olive oil = ½ cup

Samah Ben Rejeb's recipe

Peel the onion and the potatoes. Clean the parsley in a little salted water and put the peeled onion, the peeled potatoes, the cleaned parsley and the chicken breast to cook on medium heat for 15 minutes. Mix in a blender to make a smooth paste. Season, and break into this mixture two raw eggs and mix thoroughly.

Hard boil the other two eggs and dice them. Add them to the already-made stuffing. Heat the oil. On a plate spread the puff pastry sheets and proceed as for the previous recipe. The lemon is sliced to be served with the hot *briks*.

Note: Another variant uses tuna from a tin (no cooking needed), instead of chicken breast. Capers and grated cheese are added instead of potatoes.

Vegetables Cakes

Serves 4
Cooking time: 1h 20 mins

4 eggs
150g flour = 1 cup+ 3 tbsp
200g cauliflower = 1¾ cups
250g firm tomatoes = 2 cups
250g aubergine = 2 cups
250g artichokes = 2 cups
1 lemon
50g grated parmesan cheese = ½ cup
177ml olive oil = ¾ cup
2 tbsps salted butter
Salt and black pepper to taste

This recipe comes compliments of the chef at Fondoq Il Ghalla in Tunis.

Cut the cauliflower lengthwise, peel the aubergines and cut them into thin slices. Remove the artichoke leaves and slice the hearts. Boil some water. Add salt to taste and drop in all the vegetables to cook for 15 minutes. Strain the vegetables. Beat together the eggs, cheese, flour and salted butter.

Remove the seeds of the tomatoes and slice them. Mix the lemon juice and olive oil, and season with salt and black pepper. Drop all the vegetables (cauliflower, aubergine, artichoke and tomatoes) into this liquid. Leave to soak in the olive oil and lemon juice for an hour.

Take one vegetable at a time and dip them in the eggs beaten with cheese, flour and salted butter and deep-fry them in hot oil (190°C) until cooked and golden. Serve hot.

Tajins & Maaquoudas

P. 66 **Chicken Tajin**

P.68 **Tajin** with Malsouka

P.70 **Potato Maaquouda**

P.71 **Cauliflower Maaquouda**

Tajins, Maaqoudas

A varied diet cures more than the doctor

Eggs have been a part of our Mediterranean diet for millennia. Studies are still adding more to the list of benefits they bring to a healthy diet. *Tajin*s and *maaquoudas* use this source of nutrients, some of them hard to find in other foods. The many attributes of eggs earn them the title of the original superfood. To high quality protein, vitamins and minerals can be added omega-3 fatty acids and antioxidants. Most of the protein in an egg is found in the egg white, while the yolk contains healthy fat, vitamins, minerals and antioxidants. Just one boiled egg contains 40 percent of your daily vitamin D requirements, 25 percent of your daily selenium, vitamin B12, iron, iodine and phosphorus. A single egg contains six grams of protein - the building blocks of life. In addition, eggs raise levels of 'good' cholesterol, helping to reduce the risk of heart disease. They are filling and help with weight loss.

Separately eggs are among the top dietary sources of choline, which is essential for normal cell functioning and is particularly important during pregnancy to support healthy brain development in the baby. They contain antioxidants that are beneficial for the eyes as they may help counteract degenerative vision later in life including cataracts, macular degeneration and retina damage. Experts generally recommend up to seven eggs per week as part of a balanced diet for diabetics.

Some say that the *tajin* was brought to Tunisia by displaced Muslims from Andalusia, or perhaps, first taken there by Arab invaders and returned by immigrant Moors. The truth is uncertain, but the result can be seen on our kitchen tables clearly today. But note that the Tunisian *tajin* is not to be confused with the Moroccan variety which is generally a kind of stew. The Tunisian variety is like a deluxe spicy tortilla. There are spinach *tajin*s, parsley ones, and others bringing in cheese, peas, artichokes or even aubergines. Still others use grilled salad, tuna, anchovies, merguez sausage, sesame seeds, dried meat or bread. But normally just one main ingredient is at the centre of preparing a *tajin* - refrain from compiling a medley!

A mosaic from the town of Nabeul. Tunisia is home to some of the best preserved Roman mosaics in the world.

Chicken Tajin

Serves 4
Cooking time: 1h 15 mins

My signature recipe is the standard *tajin* **used all over Tunisia, tweaked here very slightly.**

2 chicken breasts (400-500g) = 0.88-1.1lbs
6 eggs
1 large potato peeled and diced (250g) = 2 cups
1 medium onion peeled and chopped (125g) = 1 cup
A handful of chickpeas (60g) = ½ cup
200g spinach chopped = 1¾ cups
100g parsley chopped = ¾ cup
2 tbsps tomato purée
3 tbsps olive oil
½ tbsp paprika
1 tsp capers
Salt and pepper to taste

First Season the chicken breasts, cover them with water and boil them for 20 minutes.

Separately, fry the chopped onion, add the tomato purée, the paprika and the chickpeas, season and cover with water. Let them cook on moderate medium heat for the time the chicken is cooking. Finely dice and fry the potatoes separately, drain them, season and keep aside. Dice the cooked chicken.

When the chicken, the sauce and the diced potatoes have been cooked and cooled, whisk the eggs thoroughly, and season. Mix in thoroughly the chicken, the sauce, the fried potatoes, the chopped spinach, the chopped parsley and the capers. Butter an ovenproof dish and pour this mixture in. In an oven preheated to 180° C, put the dish to cook for 30-40 minutes. Check after 30 minutes that the eggs are cooked by inserting a barbecue stick or similar. If it comes out dry then the dish is ready. Serve hot with a tomato sauce.

Note: This dish can be served cold for a buffet, cut up in small squares.

Tajin with Malsouka

Serves 4
Cooking time: 1h 20 mins

250g chicken (a mixture of leg and breast) = 2 cups
100g chicken liver = ¾ cup
100g beef kidneys = ¾ cup
60g chickpeas = ½ cup
6 eggs medium size
60g Gruyère cheese = ½ cup
60g Parmesan cheese = ½ cup
60g Edam cheese = ½ cup
12 sheets of *malsuqa* puff pastry
60g butter = ½ cup
3 tbsps olive oil
A pinch of saffron = ¼ tsp
Salt and pepper to taste

My cousin, Moufida Ferchichi's recipe.

Cut up and season the chicken, chicken liver and kidneys. Heat one tablespoon of olive oil and half of the butter and add the meat and chickpeas. Cover with water and bring to a boil. Then leave this to simmer on low heat for 45-50 minutes. Leave to cool. Add the diced Gruyère cheese and the Edam cheese cut into strips, along with the grated Parmesan, the two eggs which have been hard-boiled and the other four raw ones. Season with salt, pepper and the saffron and mix thoroughly.

Butter generously a square oven-proof dish. Brush with butter six of the puff pastry sheets and overlap them at the bottom of the dish. Spread the mixture over the puff pastry. Then overlap the other six sheets, already brushed with butter, on top of the stuffing. With a sharp knife make incisions to slice into squares as illustrated. Place the oven-proof dish in a moderate oven (180°C) for 20 minutes or until the pastry is cooked. Serve hot.

Potato Maaquouda

Serves 4
Cooking time: 50 mins

900g potatoes
6 eggs medium size
1 onion finely chopped (125g) = 1 cup
60g parsley chopped = ½ cup
118ml olive oil = ½ cup
½ tbsp *harissa* = ½ tbsp
½ tsp black pepper = ½ tbsp
Salt to taste

Cousin Mufida Ferchichi's recipe:

Wash and cook the potatoes in salted water so that they are soft enough to make a mash (15 minutes). Drain, peel and crush while hot. Clean the parsley and chop finely. Heat the oil and fry the onion. Dilute the *harissa* with a little water and add it to the fried onion, the potato mash, the chopped parsley and the black pepper. Break into this mixture the raw eggs and season with salt. Mix well and put in an oven-proof dish. Place in an oven preheated to 180° C and cook for about 25-30 minutes until it is golden. Before serving cut in slices and serve hot with your favourite bread.

Cauliflower Maaqouda

Serves 4
Cooking time: 50 mins

1 medium size cauliflower about 1kg = 2.2 lbs
1 onion finely chopped (125g) = 1 cup
6 eggs, 3 hard-boiled + 3 raw
2 tbsps grated parmesan cheese
60g parsley cleaned and chopped = ½ cup
118ml of olive oil = ½ cup
30g salted butter = ¼ cup
½ tbsp *harissa*
(mixed in ½ tbsp of water)
Salt and black pepper to taste

Cousin Mufida Ferchichi's recipe:

Boil two litres of water, add salt and cook the cauliflower for 15 minutes. Mix the chopped parsley, the finely chopped onion, the grated parmesan cheese and the cut up hard-boiled eggs. Add the olive oil and the salted butter, the diluted *harissa* and break in the remaining three raw eggs. Add salt and black pepper to taste. Put the mixture into an oven-proof dish and cook in a pre-heated oven to 180° C for 20 minutes or until the top is golden and a knife inserted into the pastry emerges clean. Once out of the oven cut the *maaqouda* into slices and serve hot.

Soups

P. 76 **Whole Chicken and Vegetable Soup**

P. 79 **Fish Soup from the Tunisian Sahel**

P.80 **Fish Broudou**

P.81 **Barkoukech**

P.82 **Borghol**

P.83 **White Dried Bean Soup**

P.84 **Lablabi**

P.87 **Sfax Hlelem**

Soups

There's skill in all things, even in making soup

As we all know so well, soups are filling, warming and mostly liquid - a great way to stay hydrated in winter, when it is quite common to drink less than you need. In cool weather, you still need to drink as you still lose fluid through daily activities. They also boost your immune system. Soups help to stave off colds and flu, while the warm liquid helps soothe a sore throat.

Most soups are loaded with disease-fighting nutrients. They are also a great way to regenerate produce that may be about to pass its prime - tossing them into a soup can prolong their useful life. Last but not least, soups are inexpensive, quick and easy to prepare and if you make double quantities they can be stored in the freezer to enjoy another day.

Nabeul is known for its pottery, drawing on a tradition that can be traced back to Andalusia.

Soups

Whole Chicken and Vegetable Soup

Whole chicken and vegetable soup

Serves 4
Cooking time: 2h 20 mins

1 large chicken (1kg) = 2.2 lbs
1 large onion (150g) = 1¼ cups
4 cloves garlic
200g potatoes = 1¾ cups
2 carrots (150g) = 1¼ cups
150g turnips = 1¼ cups
2 sticks celery (100g) = ¾ cup
½ a leek (70g) = ½ cup
60g Cabbage = ½ cup
50g Parsley (a handful) = ½ cup
2 tbsps olive oil
1 tsp salted butter
1½ tsp tomato paste
1½ tbsp *harissa*
Salt and pepper to taste
3 litres of water = 6.6 pints

Grandmother's Recipe

Although this dish was one of my grandmother's signature dishes I was surprised to come across it in Marseilles, Beirut and the Valencia region of Spain, albeit with some variations. So it seems to be a truly Mediterranean soup. A colleague from the London Jewish Free School told me that her mother prepared the same kind of soup when they were unwell because, like my grandmother, she believed the soup would make them better. Around November my grandmother also made this regularly to strengthen our immune system and protect against colds and influenza. She calls it 'food penicillin'.

Clean and cut up the chicken. Peel and cut the onions and the garlic. In a large cooking pot heat the oil and lightly fry the onion and garlic. Then fry the pieces of chicken. Peel, wash and cut up the vegetables: potatoes, carrots, turnips, leeks, celery, parsley and the cabbage. Add them to the chicken pot. Pour in three litres of water. Add the butter, the tomato paste, salt and pepper. Cook on low heat on hob (or in the oven at 150°C) for a couple of hours. If too thick add a little more water and bring back to a simmer. Serve hot with toasted bread.

Fish Soup from the Tunisian Sahel

Serves 4
Cooking time: 1h

1 large meaty fish, any kind (350-375g) = 3 cups
Bread (750g) = 6 cups= 1.65lbs
Juice of 1 lemon
2 tbsps olive oil
½ tbsp salted butter
Salt and pepper to taste
2 litres of water = 3.64 pints

I came across fish recipes in a number of villages in the Sahel, the region that stretches along the eastern coast of Tunisia, from Hammamet in the north to Mahdia in the south, passing the governorates of Monastir, Mahdia and Sousse. Its name derives from the Arabic word for 'shore'.

This one is from a small restaurant. I was given it by a generous cook, Mohamed Salem, in 1959.

Mix yeast, sugar and water. Cover and leave to rest for 20 minutes.

Clean the fish, cut it up into largish chunks and fry the pieces in the oil and butter. Add the water and cook on moderate medium heat for 30-40 minutes. Then drain the stock and keep the pieces of fish, making sure they are free of bones. Add the lemon juice, salt, pepper and the bread cut up. If you think the bread is too much, have less, according to taste, of course.

This is a dish for a family, designed to keep them healthily fed. In the Sahel fish is cheap and is consumed every day.

Opposite: View of Hammamet looking out to sea.

Fish Broudou

Serves 4
Cooking time: 2h 20 mins

500g fish (any kind) = 4 cups
60g kale = ½ cup
60g celery = ½ cup
150g leeks = 1 ¼ cup
150g carrots = 1 ¼ cup
150g turnips = 1 ¼ cup
175g small to medium potatoes = 1½ cup
15g parsley = 2 tbsp
2 tbsps olive oil
1 tbsp tomato paste
1 tsp of black pepper or to taste
Salt to taste
2 litres water = 3.64 pints

Another fish soup, this one is known as *broudou*

Clean the parsley and the celery and tie them to make a bouquet. Peel the carrots and turnips and cut them and the kale cut up in 2cm strips. Wash and peel the potatoes but leave them whole. Put all the prepared ingredients in a pot with the water, the olive oil, season with salt and add the tomato paste. Simmer on a low heat (or in the oven at 150°C) and leave to cook for two hours.

Clean the fish and cut into small pieces. Season with salt and black pepper and add to the pot. Cook for 20 minutes more.

Remove the bouquet of parsley and celery and throw away. Take the vegetables out and blend until smooth. Take the fish out and lightly crumble it. Serve in a tureen with the vegetables which have been puréed. Then pour the stock over them through a sieve. Check the seasoning and serve hot.

Barkoukech

Serves 4
Cooking time: 1h

- 4 slices beef stewing steak (750g in all) = 1.65 lbs (your butcher might also give you some bones to include)
- 4 dried octopus tentacles or cuttlefish (750g) = 1.65 lbs
- 4 dried little fish (600g) = 1.32lbs (chelba is popular but any small fish will do)
- 4 chicken thighs with bones (225g) = ½ lb
- 80g chickpeas = ¾ cup (dried are traditionally used, but tinned or bottled chickpeas are fine)
- 80g = ¾ cup beans dried, soaked overnight and peeled
- A handful of thick grain couscous (60g) = ½ cup
- ½ glass dried apricots (*fermess*) (100g) = ¾ cup
- 2 cloves of garlic, peeled and crushed
- 1 medium onion finely cut up (125g) =1 cup
- 3 celery stems with leaves (125g) =1 cup
- 12 Swiss chard leaves cut up in strips
- 1 piece of pumpkin diced (100g) = A little less than cup
- 2 carrots diced (125g) = 1 cup
- 1 turnip diced (125g) = 1 cup
- 4 red peppers (1kg) = 2.2 lbs
- 2 tbsps of tomato paste

continued...
- 1 tsp of paprika
- 2 tbsps of *ras el hanout*
- 1 tsp of cumin
- 250 ml of olive oil = 1 small cup

Put oil, onion, garlic, dried vegetables and meats in a pressure cooker (4-5litres size). Fry for 5 minutes mixing the ingredients. Add the spices, the red peppers, the sour apricots and the tomato paste. Fry for another five minutes. Add the fresh vegetables along with 1½ litres of water. Close the pressure cooker and leave to cook on medium heat for 40 minutes. Open the pressure cooker and add the barkoukech, a kind of very thick couscous. Season to taste. Leave to simmer. Add a little water from time to time in order to keep a consistency of soup. Ten minutes later check it is cooked and add a teaspoon of cumin powder. Serve hot.

Borghol

Serves 4
Cooking time: 1h 45 mins

150g cracked wheat = 1¼ cups
60g chickpeas from a bottle = ½ cup
2 tbsps tomato purée
2 or 3 cloves of garlic
1 tsp olive oil
½ tbsp tbsp of *harissa*
½ tsp cumin seeds
1 tsp paprika
Juice of 1 lemon
Salt to taste
2 litres of water = 3.64 pints

Kairouan cracked wheat soup.

Borghol is trimmed and crushed wheat. Traditionally the grains were boiled with salt until they burst, then sun dried, and then once more crushed in a mortar. That was in the olden days. Now *borghul* **is mostly bought in the supermarket. This is also a winter dish, but it is served in Ramadan all over North Africa.**

Mix together the cracked wheat, the chickpeas and the oil in the water and leave it to cook on moderate medium heat 175°C for about 90 minutes. Add the tomato purée, the whole peeled garlic and the paprika. Leave it to cook another 15 minutes. Add the *harissa* diluted in a bit of water and the cumin seeds. Check the salt and add the lemon juice, both to taste. Serve hot.

White Dried Bean Soup

Serves 4
Cooking time: 2h 30 mins

500g white dried beans = 4 cups
118ml olive oil = ½ cup
½ tbsp *harissa*
½ tbsp cumin seeds
2 cloves garlic crushed
2 litres water = 3.64 pints
Salt to taste

Jewish recipe from the Isle of Jerba

Soak the beans overnight. Cook them in the water for 2-3 hours. Make a purée by crushing them with a wooden spoon. Add the oil and the *harissa* diluted in a little water. Crush the garlic and the cumin seeds and add them to the broth. Add salt to taste. Leave to cook on medium heat for another 15 to 20 minutes. Serve hot.

Lablabi

Serves 4
Cooking time: 40 mins

300g chickpeas = 2½ cups
4 tbsps olive oil = ¼ cup
3 cloves garlic
½ tsp *harissa*
½ tsp cumin seeds
½ large lemon
Salt to taste

A much loved Tunisian soup suitable for vegetarians. This is another popular breakfast dish that can be traced to the Ottoman rule in Tunisia – apparently it was the staple of the Ottoman army. It is an inexpensive dish and, as it consists mainly of chickpeas, it is rich in protein, and a good source of energy. Some people like to eat theirs spicy, others refine their lablabi by adding eggs and tuna.

The old recipe uses dried chickpeas soaked overnight and cooked in 1½ litre of water until tender. This is not necessary. Chickpeas from a bottle or a tin will be as good and saves work.

Cook them for 20 minutes. Add *harissa*, the crushed garlic, cumin and salt. Leave to cook on moderate medium heat for another 20 minutes or so depending on the type of chickpeas. Sprinkle the olive oil and the lemon juice. Serve hot with left over bread.

The same recipe, replacing the chickpeas by dried white beans, is called *mdammis*.

Sfax Hlelem

Serves 4
Cooking time: 1h 20 mins

4 small pieces qadid dried meat (250g / 2 cups). (can be replaced with fresh meat)
4 merguez (250g) = 2 cups
150g *hlelem* or soup pasta = 2 cups
1 small onion (100g) = ¾ cup
1 celery stick (60g) = ½ cup
2 tbsps of olive oil
1 tsp of tomato paste
1 tsp of *harissa*
½ tsp of paprika
A handful of dried mint leaves (15g) = 2 tbsp
A handful of parsley (15g) = 2 tbsp
Salt to taste
2 litres of water = 3.64 pints

Opposite: The Grand Mosque of Sfax dates back to 849, when the city walls were also constructed.

My friend Mohsen Said's recipe.

Mohsen is from Gafsa, and his wife is Sicilian. Together they run a successful restaurant in Spain. This is his mother's recipe. Hlelem is a kind of thin hand-rolled noodle. Skilled women make them with dough for bread which they roll into thin ropes before they cut them up into pieces. Then they run them between their thumb and forefinger to give them their shape. Finally they put them out in the sun to dry over an upside down sieve. They are delicious but time consuming to make. Every region has its variant recipe. In the north fresh lamb and chickpeas are used. Other regions use spinach as well. This one is from the southern coastal town of Sfax. The tradition of hlelem making is kept alive by women working from home who make them to order. Sun dried hlelem keep for months. Outside Tunisia they are unavailable, but can be replaced by any thin soup noodle. The result is not quite the same but still good.

Hlelem arrived in Tunisia from Andalusia brought by displaced Moors who settled in Tunisia, and it quickly became very popular, especially on winter Ramadan evenings.

Heat the oil and fry the onion which has been peeled and cut in small pieces. Add in the dried meat and the merguez. Add the tomato paste, *harissa* and the paprika. Clean the parsley and the celery and cut them up. Add them to the pot. Cover with water and leave to cook on low heat. When the meat and the merguez are cooked (40-50 minutes) add 1½ litres of water and turn up the heat to cook for another 10 minutes. Crumble the dried mint leaves and add to the pot. Add the hlelem or soup pasta and leave to cook for 20 minutes. Check the seasoning and serve hot.

Pasta Dishes

P. 92 **Spaghetti with Lamb**

P. 93 **Macaroni in the Oven**

P. 95 **Sousse Beef and Tomato Macaroni**

Pasta Dishes

Eat slowly live long

Pasta is probably the most versatile foodstuff known to humanity. It was transported from China to the rest of the World by the Venetian explorer Marco Polo. Made from wheat, it is one of the basic food groups in a healthy diet.

It has a long shelf-life, comes in many different shapes and is among the few foods that may appear at any stage of the menu. Angel hair pasta appears in soups and desserts, cooks in seconds, cuts appetite, provides affordable energy and is easy to use. Other pasta shapes share most of these qualities. All they need is some olive oil tossed in a pan with black pepper, grated cheese and perhaps some sweet pepper, onion, or tomato cut up in a sauce. This versatility is dangerous, as it can encourage over-indulgence. Explore its great variety, but apply moderation. Try to use some wholegrain varieties and keep individual servings as close to one hundred grams as possible. Treated in this way it will become a family friend, affordable, easy to use in a wide range of dishes, nourishing and energizing.

Despite its carbohydrates, research has shown that people who eat pasta as part of a Mediterranean diet have a lower body mass index than those who don't, as long as you don't overdo it. They also have less belly fat. It does not have much salt, which is good for healthy heart and lower blood pressure and diabetes. It is low in fat. It has just over half a gram of fat per serving that is if you do not drench your pasta in butter, cheese or olive oil.

Opposite: *Ever versatile pasta in some of its myriad forms.*

Pasta Dishes

Spaghetti with Lamb

Serves 4
Cooking time: 1h 20 mins

500g leg of lamb = 1 lb 2 oz
500g spaghetti = 1 lb 2 oz.
60g chickpeas = ½ cup
100g raisins = ¾ cup
1 onion (100g) = ¾ cup
2 tbsps salted butter
2 tbsps olive oil
2 eggs
2 tbsps tomato paste
½ tbsp paprika
½ tbsp black pepper or to taste
Salt to taste

My sister Zohra's recipe.

Cut up the meat in chunk size pieces to your liking. Season with salt and black pepper and fry in the oil with the onion which has been finely cut up. Add the chickpeas, the tomato paste and the paprika. Cover with just enough water, cook on moderate hot heat and then lower the heat to simmer for 90 minutes.

Take the pieces of meat off the heat and set to one side. Add one litre of water to the pot and boil. Put a couscous pot on top of the stock and put in the spaghetti to steam. When it is soft throw it into the stock with the raisins and cook for 10 minutes.

Add the salted butter, check the seasoning and remove from heat. Leave to rest a few minutes. Serve the spaghetti decorated with the pieces of lamb and the hard-boiled eggs in slices

Macaroni in the Oven

Serves 4
Cooking time: 1h 45 mins

500g diced beef = 4 cups
500g macaroni = 1 lb 2 oz
100g dried white beans (soaked overnight) = ¾ cup
6 eggs (of which 4 hard-boiled)
1 chopped onion (100g) = ¾ cup
3 cloves of garlic
3 tbsps tomato paste
2 tbsps grated parmesan cheese
60g Gruyère cheese = ½ cup
2 tbsps salted butter
½ cup olive oil
A pinch of saffron = ¼ tsp
Salt and black pepper to taste

My recipe.

Dice the beef, walnut size, season with salt, black pepper and saffron. Heat the oil and fry the beef gently with the chopped onion and the crushed garlic. Add the tomato paste and the dried white beans that have been soaked overnight. Cover with water and simmer on a low heat for about an hour or until the beef and the beans are cooked. Take off the heat and leave to cool.

Add the grated Parmesan cheese, the Gruyère cheese diced small and four hard-boiled eggs (peeled and sliced) and add two raw eggs. Season and mix well.

In a large pot boil salted water. Cook the macaroni in the boiling salted water for 10 minutes or what the instructions on the packet say. Drain and, in a buttered oven-proof dish mix the macaroni with the beef dish and the cheeses. Pre-heat the oven to 180° C and put the dish to cook for 15 minutes or until golden. Serve hot.

Sousse Beef and Tomato Macaroni

Serves 4
Cooking time: 2h 30 mins

500g stewing steak roughly diced = 1 lb 2 oz
500g macaroni = 1 lb 2 oz
1 large onion chopped (175g) = 1½ cups
5 cloves garlic finely chopped
2 tbsps cumin
4 tbsps tomato purée
2 tbsps olive oil
1 tbsp parsley
Salt and pepper to taste

My sister Zohra's recipe.

Heat the oil and fry the chopped onion and the finely chopped garlic. Do not let them burn, but they should lightly brown. Add the roughly diced meat. Seal the meat in the hot pan and then add the tomato purée, followed by the cumin. Season and cover the meat with water.

Leave to cook on low heat (or in the over at 165°C) for two hours. A quarter of an hour before the meat has finished cooking put salted water in a large pot to boil. Then throw in the macaroni to cook for 10 minutes. When *al dente* drain and add it to the meat to cook for 2-3 minutes. Mix thoroughly, add the chopped parsley, check the seasoning and serve hot with your choice of steamed vegetable on the side.

Salads

P. 100 **Slata Mechouia**

P.102 **Slata Tunisia - Fresh Tunisian Salad**

P.105 **Slatit Blankit**

P.107 **Omok Houria**

P.108 **Radish Salad**

P. 109 **Anchovy Salad**

P.109 **Fennel Salad**

P.111 **Fricassée**

P.113 **Slatit Fondouq El Ghalla**

P.114 **La Goulette Octopus**

Salads

A salad a day keeps disease and ageing at bay

'A diet rich in vegetables and fruits can lower blood pressure, reduce risk of heart disease and stroke, prevent some types of cancer, lower risk of eye and digestive problems, and have a positive effect upon blood sugar which can help keep appetite in check'.
Article in the Harvard Public Health Review

Aside from natural good taste, crunchy texture, wonderful colours and fragrances, a large serving of fresh, uncooked vegetable and leaves each day has significant health benefits.

Brightly coloured fruits and vegetables in the 'red' family are of particular benefit. This includes produce with orange, purple, red or burgundy flesh. The obvious examples are tomatoes, red and orange peppers, carrots, and pomegranates. All of these have substantial positive effects, from antioxidant through to anti-inflammatory benefits on the body, and are used across Tunisian cuisine. And they look appetizing as well.

Tunisians are in the habit of consuming salads daily throughout the year. They are a natural source of fibre that helps to reduce cholesterol and blood sugar levels. Adequate fibre intake helps with weight loss and healthy weight maintenance. It provides protection from bowel disease. The presence of vitamin K in raw vegetables is linked to low bone mineral density in women. Lettuce and carrots help the eyes to filter out high intensity light levels. Lettuce and spinach help preserve muscles including heart muscle. Salads have an extra capacity to improve skin tone. Extra antioxidants can be included in your oil-based salad dressings by adding garlic and herbs such as basil, parsley or coriander. Be sure to use olive oil, because it assists the breakdown and absorption of nutrients.

Raw nuts are also used in salads and nibbled before meals, helping to satisfy hunger and control weight.

Salads

Slata Mechouia

Serves 4
Cooking time: 1h

2 hard-boiled eggs
2 onions (200g) = 1¾ cups
200g of tomatoes = 1¾ cups
200g sweet green peppers = 1¾ cups
60g hot green peppers = ½ cup
100g tinned tuna fish = ¾ cup
1 tbsp capers
4 tbsps olive oil to taste
Juice of 1 lemon
Salt and pepper to taste

Grilled Tunisian salad – *Slata mechouia* – **grandmother's recipe.**

This smoky-tasting salad is an ubiquitous starter dish, sometimes also served to accompany other dishes. It is more like a grilled vegetable sauce than a salad. In the month of Ramadan it is served almost every day.

Start by grilling the tomatoes, hot and sweet peppers. Peel them when hot and remove the seeds. Peel the onions and grill them. Cut all the ingredients in small pieces. Add the lemon juice and mix. Season with salt and pepper to taste. Drizzle olive oil generously over the vegetables.

Decorate with the tuna in pieces and the hard-boiled eggs in slices. Serve cold.

Slata Tunsia
Fresh Tunisian Salad

Serves 4
Cooking time: 40 mins

Grandmother's recipe. This recipe is always a hit. It is served with lots of dishes but also used in sandwiches.

200g tomatoes = 1¾ cups
200g green peppers = 1¾ cups
100g onions = ¾ cup
100g apples = ¾ cup
60g black olives = ½ cup
100g tuna fish from tin = ¾ cup
100g white cheese (could use feta) = ¾ cup
½ tbsp dry mint to sprinkle
4tbsps olive oil
2 tbsps any white vinegar
Salt and pepper to taste

Wash the tomatoes and peppers and remove the seeds. Peel the onions and the apples. Cut all ingredients into small pieces. Add the mint leaves and the vinegar. Season with salt and pepper to taste. Sprinkle generously with olive oil and the shredded tuna.

Spoon into a serving dish. Decorate with the olives and the shredded feta cheese. Serve cold.

Slatit Blankit

Serves 4
Cooking time: 30 mins

500g of slices of baguette or any left over bread that is to hand =1.1lbs
100g tuna fish = ¾ cup
2 hard-boiled eggs
100g hard cheese (Gruyère or similar) = ¾ cup
60g black olives = ½ cup
60g capers = ½ cup
3 tbsps olive oil
2 tbsps vinegar
½ tbsp *harissa*
Salt and pepper to taste.

Bread Salad – Aunt Fatma's recipe.

Slice the bread 1cm (¾ inch) thick. Hard boil the eggs and slice them so that you can see the yoke in the middle of the hard white. Shred the tuna, take the stones out from the olives and dice the cheese. In a large soup plate dilute the *harissa* in a little water, add to it the olive oil and the vinegar and season with salt and pepper. In this mixture soak the slices of bread one by one turning them on the side that is still dry so that they soak all the liquid. When the slices of bread have absorbed all the liquid place it on a serving dish until you get all them nicely filling the dish. On each slice put one slice of egg, a bit of the shredded tuna, a few cubes of cheese, some slices of olives and some capers.

Serve cold as a starter or as canapés.

Omok Houria

Serves 4
Cooking time: 30 mins

500g carrots =1 lb 2 oz
100g white cheese (fetta) = ¾ cup
4 tbsps olive oil
2 tbsps vinegar
2 cloves garlic
½ tbsp *harissa*
10g green olives = 1½ tbsp
10g black olives = 1½ tbsp
10g capers
½ tsp caraway seeds
Salt and pepper to taste
For decoration: 6 green and 6 black olives, pitted.

Carrot salad - my signature dish.

This dish accompanies all my buffets. My friends know it well and look forward to it. No matter how much I make all gets consumed. This recipe is for four people but I hope you will not think me mean. You can always make more if you, too, decide that it is to your liking. By the way this dish is called *omok houria* **(literal meaning: Your mother is a mermaid), and its bewitching taste hints that she is a bit of a genie. Its ingredients are boiled and mashed carrots, seasoned with spices and** *harissa* – **the ideal vegan dish, until hard-boiled eggs or tuna are added.**

Peel the carrots and cut them to 1cm (¾ inch) thick rounds. Boil water in a pot and throw them in to boil. **Do not put salt in at this stage.** Wait until the carrots are really tender, then drain, season and blend the carrots into a smooth purée. Now add salt and pepper.

Dilute the *harissa* in a tablespoon of water, peel and crush the garlic. Mix these and the caraway seeds, the vinegar and oil with the mashed carrots. Put in a serving dish and decorate with olives and the cheese (either diced or cut in long strips). Cover and put in the fridge to cool. Serve chilled with pita bread or Arabic bread.

Radish Salad

Serves 4
Cooking time: 15 mins

300g radishes or beetroot = 2½ cups
10g parsley = 1½ tbsp
10g celery = 1½ tbsp
60g black olives = ½ cup
3 tbsps of olive oil
Juice of 1 small lemon
Salt and pepper to taste

Mother's recipe.

Wash and slice the radishes. Wash and finely chop the parsley and the celery. Put these in a serving dish. Add lemon juice and olive oil, and season with salt and pepper. Decorate with olives. Serve cold.

Grandmother's love for cooking and her belief in varying the family diet led her to create new dishes by changing one or two ingredients. For instance she replaces radishes with courgettes. For this she would seed and boil slightly in salted water making a purée. The rest of the recipe remains the same as the above except for adding half a teaspoon of caraway seeds and decorating her dish with small cubes of white cheese.

Anchovy Salad

Serves 4
Cooking time: 10 mins

150g anchovy fillets (3 small tins) = 1¼ cups
2 hard-boiled eggs
28g finely chopped parsley = 1oz
40g of well-cleaned capers = 1½ oz
80g black olives = 2½ oz
Juice of 1 lemon
½ cup olive oil

Drain the oil from the anchovies. Make sure you do not break the fillets. Align the anchovies on a large plate. Sprinkle the parsley. Add the well-cleaned capers. Slice the hard-boiled eggs and decorate the dish placing them between the fillets of anchovies. Drizzle with olive oil and lemon juice. Serve

Fennel Salad

Serves 4
Cooking time: 10 mins

750g fennel bulbs = 1.65lbs
25g finely chopped parsley = 1oz
50g black olives = 2oz
½ cup olive oil
2 tbsps white vinegar
Salt and black pepper to taste

Remove the fennel leaves, clean and chop or grate the fennel bulbs. Put them in a salad bowl and sprinkle the finely chopped parsley. Season with salt and black pepper. Add the olive oil, the vinegar, and the black olives and mix well. Serve.

Fricassée

Serves 4
Cooking time: 2h

For the bun:
500g white flour = 1.1lbs
1 tbsp of active dried yeast
1 tbsp of sugar
½ tbsp of salt
1 medium size egg
1 tbsp of *boukha* or vodka
3 tbsps of olive oil
250 ml of water = 1 cup

For the filling:
1 tbsp of smoked *harissa* or more if you like it hot
Tirshi (75g) = ½ cup
Preserved lemon 8g = 3 oz
Tuna (37g) = ¼ cup
1 egg
A handful of black juicy pitted olives
Capers

This belongs within the fast developing genre of street food and is one of the most popular snacks in the country. It is also inexpensive. Basically a bread bun filled with typical Tunisian ingredients, a fricassée may be varied to suit your tastes or the contents in your fridge. If you want to avoid the trouble of making the bun, just use baguette instead. This particular recipe is Jewish and uses a modest quantity of alcohol, *boukha* or vodka.

For the bun:
Place the flour, yeast, sugar and salt in a bowl and mix. This can be done by hand or using the bread kneading attachment in a blender. Add the oil and egg and continue to knead for a further minute. Add the water gradually, and knead for another five minutes. You should get dough that is a bit sticky, but soft and pleasant to touch. Add the alcohol and knead for four more minutes. Then place the dough on a well-floured surface, and form a ball. Put it in a bowl, cover with a kitchen towel and wait until it doubles its size. This should happen after one hour in a warm kitchen or longer in a cool one.

Cut small squares 8 cm^2 (3¼ inch) from greaseproof paper and spread some flour on top of them. Take the dough and, flouring it well, roll it flat until 1.5-2 cm (0.6-0.8') thick. Using a cup press circles out of the flat dough and place the greaseproof paper on top. Cover with a towel and leave to rise for another 30 minutes.

Heat the olive oil in a deep frying pan. Transfer the greaseproof paper with the dough directly into the oil. The paper will detach as soon as it comes into contact with the oil. Remove it. When the bottom side of the dough is brown, turn the dough onto the other side to brown.

It's easier to cut it when it's very hot. Use a towel to hold

Fricassée

To make tirshi or torshi:
75g pumpkin = 2.6 oz
1 tsp *harissa* = 1 tsp
1 clove crushed garlic
Juice of ½ lemon
½ tsp ground caraway seeds = ½ tsp
Salt to taste

it, cut it open, as you would for a sandwich. Leave to rest and turn your attention to making the filling.

For the filling:
Roast the diced pumpkin in a medium oven at 180°C for 20-25 minutes until soft. With a fork squash the pumpkin. Add the *harissa*, the crushed garlic, the lemon juice, the grounded caraway and salt.

To make preserved lemon paste:
1 lemon
1 tsp of brown sugar
1 1tsp of olive oil
Grind the lemon with the brown sugar and the olive oil to a fantastic paste. This paste can enrich any sandwich. You can have some in the fridge ready to use when needed.

For a perfect medium soft-boiled egg: boil water in a small pan, when the water is boiling put the egg carefully in the water and cook for 8 minutes, Put it in under a cold tap to stop the cooking process.

Note: There is no strict recipe for fricassee. Some people add slata mechouia (see recipe, page 100) and/or pickles.

Slatit Fondouq El Ghalla

Serves 4
Cooking time: 40 mins

This salad is called Fondouq II Ghalla which means 'vegetable market' and uses a mixture of vegetables, olives, capers, parsley and more. It makes a complete summer lunch meal.

250g potatoes = 0.55lbs
250g carrots = 0.55lbs
100g peas = 3.5 oz
250g artichokes = 0.55lbs
100g Dutch cheese = 3.5 oz
28g parsley = 1oz
28g capers = 1oz
28g black olives = 1oz
28g green olives = 1oz
1 lemon
½ cup olive oil
Salt and black pepper to taste

Wash the potatoes and boil them in water. Then peel and slice them.

Clean the artichokes, discard their leaves, and cook the hearts in boiling water. Shell the peas, peel the carrots and slice them. Cook them in boiling water. Mix together all the cooked ingredients and season with salt and black pepper to taste.

Place in a salad bowl and sprinkle the finely chopped parsley over them. Add the olive oil and the juice from the lemon, the capers, the olives and the sliced Dutch cheese. Serve cold.

La Goulette Octopus

Serves 4
Cooking time: 50 mins

2 large octopus tentacles (750g) = 1.65 lbs
2 large tomatoes chopped (200g) = 1¾ cup
1 small onion finely chopped (75g) = 5oz
28g finely chopped parsley = 1oz
1 lemon
2 big cloves of garlic
½ tsp coriander powder
½ tsp caraway powder
2 dried bay leaves
Salt and black pepper to taste
Olive oil to taste

The first step is to put the octopus tentacles in a pot and cover them with water. Add the bay leaves, half the lemon, the coriander powder, the caraway powder and the crushed cloves of garlic. Boil for 40 minutes. Check it is cooked by inserting a sharp knife into the meat. If it comes out clean, the octopus is cooked. Otherwise give it a few more minutes. Cut it into thin slices.

In a large serving dish mix the finely chopped parsley, the finely chopped onion, the chopped tomatoes and the thinly sliced octopus. Season with the following: the other half of the lemon, olive oil to your liking, salt and black pepper to taste. Serve.

Note: Be aware of the danger that octopus can be too salty, so taste before seasoning the way you usually do.

Fish

P. 121 **Poisson Complet**

P.122 **La Goulette Fish Cakes**

P.123 **Le Kram Fish Stew**

P.124 **Stuffed Squid**

P.125 **Octopus with Garlic**

Fish

Better a small fish than an empty dish.

In Tunisia, fish is not only used in cooking. It also appears in amulets, pendants, key chains, decorative objects. It can be seen everywhere. It was associated among the Phoenicians with the cult of Tanit, the Carthaginian Goddess, and it represented luck and prolific abundance. As we know, in early Christian religion, the fish was a symbol used for secret recognition among the Christians pursued by the Romans while, in the Jewish religion, it protected against the evil eye. Later the Muslims made it the sign of vigilance because fish never close their eyes. By extension, it was taken for granted that fish keeps the evil eye away and brings good luck. Moreover, during wedding ceremonies from the north in Bizerta to Sfax in the sourth, the groom turns several times around the largest fish his family can afford to ward off the evil eye and bring good luck into his future home.

With 1,400 km of coastline, Tunisia has excellent fresh seafood, including grouper, sea bass, red mullet, mackerel, sardines, sole, turbot, whiting, bream, perch, calamari, squid and octopus. Tunisians' consumption of fish and seafood is high. On average, a Tunisian eats fish at least once a week. Favoured seasonings are garlic, saffron, cumin, paprika and turmeric, though often fish is simply grilled with lemon and olive oil or fried in olive oil and served as it is. It is also baked and stuffed with herbs. Tasty fish brochettes are popular, known as kebabs. Succulent large prawns are grilled, sautéd with garlic, parsley or simmered in a clay pot. Mostly are eaten freshly caught the same day. Others are preserved. The traditional accompaniment for fried fish is *tastira*, a delicate mixture of chopped fried tomatoes and eggs seasoned with caraway seeds, salt and olive oil.

*A Roman mosaic (**below**), found in the town of Dougga and depicting Odysseus, the great seafarer, lashed to the mast and resisting the call of the Sirens.*

Poisson Complet

Serves 4
Cooking time: 50 mins

4 whole fish 650g (any of the above mentioned variety) = 1.45 lbs
4 eggs
4 green hot peppers (500g) = 1 lb
2 courgettes sliced (250g) = ½ lb
Vegetable oil for frying
Green salad with vinaigrette to taste

For the chips:
1kg potatoes = 2.2 lbs
Vegetable oil for frying
Salt to taste

For the tastira:
3 green hot peppers (375g) = 13 oz
4 green peppers (Italian style) (625g) = 40 oz
6 tomatoes (quartered and seeded) (500g) = 32 oz
3 crushed cloves of garlic
3 tsps ground cumin
2 cups olive oil
Salt to taste

This legendary dish is called complete because it consists of the whole fish, accompanying carbohydrate, vegetables and a fried egg. The fish too, is usually fried but it can also be grilled. It is served in coastal restaurants all over Tunisia but its home is in La Goulette, the north-east suburb of Tunis, which is proud of its *poisson complet*. Formerly the best restaurant in which to eat it was Bichi in La Goulette. Some swore that it was among the 'seven wonders of the modern world'. That was perhaps an exaggeration, but its clientele came from all over to experience this essential Tunisian dish. A variety of fishes are used: mullet, red mullet, sea bass, sea bream, sole or tuna. This recipe uses *tastira*, which is grilled green peppers and tomatoes *(see below)*. Alternatively with grilled salad, *(see recipe, page 100)*.

Wash the vegetables and dry them. Slice the courgettes. Heat the oil. Fry the hot peppers for a few minutes on both sides. Set aside. Fry the courgettes until they are soft. Put them on a kitchen towels to dry and season with salt and pepper and set aside.

To make the tastira: Pour the vegetable oil into a frying pan on a medium heat. Fry the Italian style long peppers, then the hot peppers until the skin is blistered. Put aside. Now fry the tomatoes for five minutes. Peel and seed the peppers. Shred the tomatoes and peppers using a sharp knife so that you do not end up with a paste and what you are left with is recognisable as tomatoes and peppers.

In another frying pan heat the oil and gently fry the garlic. Add the minced tomatoes and peppers and mix them. Simmer these for just over five minutes and add the cumin and season with salt. Cover and continue to simmer for another couple of minutes. Stir a few times, but make sure the liquid is reduced. Set aside.

To fry the fish: In a large frying pan put enough oil to heat. Fry the fish for a few minutes on each side until they are golden brown. Place them on paper towels and set aside.

Chips: Peel the potatoes and wash them. Cut them into sticks the thickness desired. Dry them well. In a frying pan heat enough oil for frying on medium high heat. Fry the potato chips for ten minutes in two batches in order not to overload the pan. Let them cool while you are cooking the rest of the dish. Make sure to fry them again for a couple of minutes to crisp them up. Season with salt.

Now fry the eggs and season with salt and pepper.

Assemble dish: In a large dish place the fish in the centre. Around it put three tablespoons of tastira, three tablespoons of courgettes, green salad, some chips, an egg and a fried hot pepper. Serve hot.

La Goulette Fish Cakes

Serves 4
Cooking time: 30 mins

250g sea bream = 16 oz
1 small onion (75g) = 5 oz
2 cloves garlic
1 egg
60g parsley = 4 oz
3 tbsps olive oil
3 tbsps bread crumbs
1 tbsp cinnamon
Salt and pepper to taste

Jackie's recipe (Tunisian Jewish recipe).

Clean the fish thoroughly, cut into manageable chunks and put in a blender.

Finely chop the onion, garlic, parsley and put these in the blender as well until smooth. Season with salt, pepper, cinnamon and add the beaten egg. Take the mixture out of the blender and between your hands make disks of 7cm (2¾ inches) in diameter and 1cm (½ inch) thick. Sprinkle the bread crumbs over the fish cakes. Preheat the oil and fry them until golden. Serve hot with a tomato sauce, new potatoes and green beans or your favourite vegetable.

Le Kram Fish Stew

Serves 4
Cooking time: 45 mins

500g of sea bass = 1 lb 2 oz
500g tomatoes wash and chop = 1 lb 2 oz
1 large onion peel and chop (125g) = 8 oz
2 tbsps tomato paste
½ courgette wash and chop (100g) = 6 oz
½ green pepper wash and chop (75g) = 5 oz
Aubergine washed and chopped (75g) = 5 oz
1 chilli finely chopped (15g) = ½ oz
3 tbsps olive oil
1 tbsp capers
½ tbsp raisins
1 tbsp basil washed and chopped
500ml fish stock = 2 cups
Salt and pepper to taste
2 cloves garlic peeled
4 slices bread to toast (85g) = 3 oz

Rabia's recipe.

Wash, clean and cut up the fish. Heat two of the three tablespoons of olive oil and fry the already chopped onion, then the chopped courgette, pepper, aubergine, the chilli and the chopped the tomatoes.

Let cook for one minute, then add the tomato paste and cook for another two minutes. Add the fish stock, capers, raisins and the sea bass and cook for 15 minutes. Throw in the basil, salt and pepper to taste and check that the fish is cooked but not over cooked. Serve with the other tablespoon of olive oil drizzled over the top, along with the toasted bread with the garlic rubbed on.

Stuffed Squid

Serves 4
Cooking time: 45 mins

4 small squid (500g) = 1 lb 2 oz
2 eggs
1 slice of bread made into crumbs - stale fine (38g) = 1½ oz
60g parsley = 4 oz
1 tbsp olive oil
1 tsp *harissa*
½ tsp paprika
Salt and black pepper to taste

My sister Zohra's recipe

Clean the squid thoroughly inside and out. Remove the squid bodies and set aside. Finely chop the tentacles, the parsley and add the breadcrumbs. Add to this mixture one tablespoon of olive oil and add the eggs. Season the mixture with salt, black pepper and paprika and use it to stuff the bodies of the squid.

Sew the openings in the bodies with a needle. Cook them in a spicy tomato sauce and serve the dish with seasonal vegetables.

Octopus with Garlic

Serves 4
Cooking time: 1h

1kg octopus = 2.2 lbs
1 medium onion (100g) = 7 oz
1 tbsp tomato paste
1 tsp *harissa*
½ tbsp paprika
1 whole garlic head (40g) = 1½ oz
½ tsp coriander powder
½ cup olive oil = 4 oz
Salt and black pepper to taste

Wash the octopus well. Remove the eyes and the mouth. With a rolling pin beat it to tenderize the flesh. Wash again and drain. Slice the tentacles and the body and season with salt, black pepper and coriander.

Finely chop the onion. Heat the oil and brown the pieces of octopus and the onion. Add the tomato paste, the *harissa* and the paprika. Cover with water and bring to the boil in a covered pan. Lower the heat and simmer gently for five minutes or until tender. It may need a few more minutes.

While the octopus is simmering peel the garlic and crush it. Add them to the pot 30 minutes before the end of the cooking. Serve hot.

Octopus with cumin or *Kammouniya bil quarnit*: Same recipe as above. Replace the garlic with one tablespoon of cumin seeds.

Meat Dishes

P. 130 **Kairouan Stuffed Chicken**

P.132 **Tunis Walnut Chicken**

P.133 **Kairouan Chicken with Almond Sauce**

P.134 **Rice in the Oven with Chicken**

P.135 **Marinated Lamb Cutlets**

P. 136 **Leg of Lamb Roasted with Artichokes**

P.138 **Kifta Bil Salsa**

P.140 **Kairouan Winter Dish Lamb with Spinach**

P.142 **Stuffed Beef Sirloin**

P.143 **Tahfifa**

Meat

*Eat according to your own taste,
but dress in accordance with other people's tastes*

Chicken has many health benefits. It provides vitamins and minerals involved in brain function. Dark and white chicken meat contain vitamin B12 and choline, which together may promote brain development in children, help the nervous system function properly and aid cognitive performance in older adults. Chicken contains tryptophan, an amino acid linked with mood, responsible for raising serotonin levels in your brain. Serotonin is a 'feel-good' neuro-chemical influence, linked with mood which also strengthens bones. Dieticians claim that chicken makes a vital low-fat, low-cholesterol contribution to the family diet.

Tunisian women believe it fights colds. My grandmother always gave it us to when we were suffering from a cold. Chicken soup may restore fluids, loosen mucus in the chest and provides optimal nutrients like zinc and protein to strengthen the natural immune system. On top of these medicinal benefits it is used to aid weight loss and lower blood sugar levels. Aside from all of that, it is famously tasty and mixes easily with a range of vegetables and pulses.

Chicken is a versatile source of protein, but has to be thoroughly cooked. Raw chicken should not be washed before cooking and should always be cooked at a minimum temperature of 75°C / 170°F.

*A Roman Mosaic **(opposite)**, now in the Bardo National Museum, depicts Diana, the Huntress, about to dispatch a gazelle.*

Meat

Kairouan Stuffed Chicken

Serves 4
Cooking time: 1 hr

1 chicken (1½ kilos) = 3.3 lbs
Minced meat (150g) = 9 oz
Rice 1 cup = 8 oz
1 tomato, chopped (125g) = 8 oz
A handful of pine nuts (14g) = ½ oz
3 cups water (500ml). = 1½ pint
A pinch of cinnamon = ¼ tsp
Salt and pepper to taste

Clean out the chicken cavity and rub it with a bit of flour to absorb any taste which does not belong. Rinse the flour, dry and season the cavity ready for stuffing.

In a bowl mix the minced lamb, the rice, the chopped tomato, the pine nuts, cinnamon and season with salt and pepper and add a half cup of water. Fill both the body and neck cavities and sew them shut.

In a pressure cooker place the chicken with the rest of the water (2½ cups), salt to taste and boil for 30 minutes. Check that it is cooked through by piercing the skin with a skewer. Carve and serve hot.

My neighbour Jamila adds a stick of cinnamon, a handful of rice and a handful of parsley to the water and stews it to serve as soup before the main dish of stuffed chicken, a family-friendly dish for a winter day.

Tunis Walnut Chicken

Serves 4
Cooking time: 1h 10 mins

This is Nargis' family recipe. She once served it cold in a buffet. Another time she brought it to a picnic in the country.

- 1 chicken (1½ kilos) = 3.3 lbs
- 2 slices bread (40g) = 6 oz
- 200g walnuts = 2 cups
- 1 medium carrot (75g) = 5 oz
- 1 medium onion (75g) = 5 oz
- 2 tbsps fresh coriander
- 1 tbsp paprika
- 1 litre of water = 4¼ cups
- Salt and pepper to taste

Chop the meat into large chunks and cook in the seasoned water in a pressure cooker for 30 minutes. Add the parsley, the onion and the carrot which have been peeled and cut in pieces. Let the chicken cool in the broth. Skin and debone the chicken and cut it in pieces. Keep the broth.

Grind the walnuts, and season with paprika. Through a cheesecloth extract the oil which you will use later to decorate the dish.

Now soak the slices of bread in the chicken broth, and then squeeze them dry and add them to the walnut/paprika paste in order to make it thicker. If you want a smoother consistency you can put this mixture in a blender.

Place the cut up chicken on a serving dish on top of which you spread the walnut/soaked bread/paprika paste and finally the walnut/paprika oil is drizzled as a decoration. This dish is served hot.

Kairouan Chicken with Almond Sauce

Serves 4
Cooking time: 1h

1 chicken cut in pieces (1kg) = 2.2 lbs
1 medium onion finely chopped (100g) = 7 oz
1 clove garlic crushed
1½ tbsps olive oil
1½ tbsps fresh coriander chopped
1½ tbsps lemon juice
60g ground almonds = 4 oz
2 cups boiling water, enough to cover the chicken = 1 pint
1 chicken stock cube
1 cinnamon stick
1 pinch saffron = ¼ tsp
1 tsp ground ginger =
1½ tsps finely chopped parsley
1½ tsps grilled and halved almonds
Salt and pepper to taste

For the rice:
1 cup rice = 8 oz
2 cups water = 1 pint
1 tsp salt or to taste
1 pinch saffron   = ¼ tsp

Grandmother's recipe.

In a large frying pan heat the olive oil and fry the chopped onion and then the crushed garlic until golden. Remove them from the pan and fry the pieces of chicken in the oil, a few at a time, stirring all the while until the chicken is golden on all sides. Add the saffron and the ground ginger. Then cover the chicken with water and add the cinnamon stick, the lemon juice and the chicken stock. Finally season with salt and pepper. Lower the heat and leave to simmer for 35-40mns. Add the chopped fresh coriander and continue simmering for another 10-12 minutes. Put the chicken in an oven-proof serving dish and keep it warm.

Discard the cinnamon stick and check you have enough stock, (at least two cups). In a small separate pan heat the ground almonds, stirring all the while until they become golden, but not brown. Remove from the heat and slowly pour in the hot stock. Simmer for 5-7 minutes. Pour the resulting thick sauce onto the chicken. Decorate with the finely chopped parsley, a few whole sprigs of parsley and the halved and grilled almonds. It is usually served hot with saffron rice, cooked separately.

Rice
Wash the rice thoroughly. Add the water, salt and pinch of saffron which had been diluted in a teaspoon of warm water. Bring to the boil. Low the heat to simmer cook for 15 minutes or until all the water has been absorbed and the grains are fluffy. Do not overcook as it becomes mushy and is ruined.

Rice in the Oven with Chicken

Serves 4
Cooking time: 1h

500g chicken breast without bones = 1 lb 2 oz
500g rice = 1 lb 2 oz
4 eggs
1 chopped onion (80g) = ¾ cups
1 tsp tomato paste
25g parsley = 1 oz
2 tbsps grated parmesan cheese
4 tbsps grated gruyere cheese = ¼ cup
2 tbsps salted butter
½ cup olive oil (118ml)
A pinch of saffron = ¼ tsp
Salt and black pepper to taste

Dice the chicken breast, pieces the size of a walnut, season them with salt and black pepper. Heat the oil and fry in it the chopped onion and the diced chicken breast. Add the tomato paste, the finely chopped parsley, cover with water and leave to cook on low heat simmering for about 30mns until the chicken is cooked.

In boiling salted water cook the rice. Drain it. Put it in a large oven proof dish on which you pour the chicken and the sauce and leave to cool. Break the eggs and add them to the rice, the sauce and the chicken as well as the cheeses, the salted butter and the pinch of saffron which had been diluted in a little water. Mix all the ingredients. Flatten the top of the dish and place the dish in a pre-heated oven at 180° C degrees for 15 to 20mns. Serve.

Marinated Lamb Cutlets

Serves 4
Cooking time: 50 mins

Narjes's recipe

For the lamb cutlets
12 lamb cutlets (1kg) = 2.2 lbs
1 tsp olive oil
1 clove crushed garlic
1 tsp ground ginger
½ tsp cumin
½ tsp paprika
Salt and pepper to taste

For the marinade:
1 medium chopped onion = 5 oz
2 cloves crushed garlic
100g fresh coriander chopped = 7 oz
100g parsley chopped = 7 oz
1 tsp lemon juice
1 tsp lemon zest
2 tbsps olive oil
1 tsp cumin
Salt and pepper to taste

Start by taking off most of the fat from the chops and tenderise them with a mallet. Mix the garlic, ginger, cumin, paprika and seasoning and rub them into the chops. Leave them to soak up their flavour into the chops for 30/40mns. Then mix the ingredients of the marinade in a bowl which you keep aside. Fry the chops in a preheated frying pan with the olive oil for a couple of minutes on each side. They must not be overcooked. Serve them hot on a bed of rice with saffron and the marinade poured all over. (See recipe for cooking rice at the bottom of recipe for Kairouan Chicken p. 135).

Leg of Lamb Roasted with Artichokes

Serves 4
Cooking time: 1h 10 mins

Grandmother's recipe

750g leg of lamb = 1.6 lbs
1kg artichokes = 2.2 lbs
1 lemon
A pinch of rose buds in powder = ¼ tsp
½ tsp cinnamon
A pinch of saffron = ¼ tsp
60g salted butter = 4 oz
Salt and black pepper to taste

Season the leg of lamb with salt, black pepper, cinnamon and rosebuds in powder. Place it in an oven-proof dish. Put the washed artichokes which had been trimmed and quartered around the leg of lamb. Dilute the saffron in a little water. Add the melted salted butter and the juice of the lemon. Sprinkle this mixture onto the leg of lamb and the quartered artichokes.

Put the dish to roast in an already heated medium oven 180° C for about 45 minutes. When ready take out from the oven, slice the leg and serve hot with the artichokes and either rice or potatoes.

Note: Instead of a leg, shoulder can be used.

Kifta Bil Salsa

Serves 4
Cooking time: ##

500g lamb shoulder = 1 lb 2 oz
250g minced lamb = 8.8 oz
500g potatoes = 1 lb 2 oz
100g tin chickpeas are fine = 3.5 oz
2 chopped onions (200g) = 7 oz
2 eggs
4 crushed cloves garlic
100g parsley finely chopped = 3.5 oz
2 tbsps tomato paste = 2 tbsp
60g rice = ½ cup
½ tsp *harissa* = ½ tbsp
½ cup of olive oil (118ml) = 4 fl oz
1 tsp cayenne pepper = 1 tsp
Salt and black pepper to taste

My cousin Mufida Ferchichi recipe for lamb meatballs.

Cut the lamb into equal size pieces, season with salt and black pepper. In a cooking pot heat the oil and fry in the seasoned lamb pieces and the chopped onions for 5 to 10mns. Add the tomato paste which had been diluted in a little water, the cayenne pepper, the *harissa*, and the chickpeas, mix all the ingredients, cover with water and bring to boil. Lower the heat. Put the lid on the pot and simmer for about 1 hour. Stir every so often and check that there is enough liquid for the sauce. If not add some to immerse the lamb.

While the meat sauce is cooking, turn your attention to the rice: Cook it in salted boiling water (double the volume of rice in the pot), simmer until dry (approximately 10 minutes). Add the rice to the crushed garlic (in a pinch of salt) and the chopped onions. Mix these ingredients with the minced lamb, season with salt, pepper to taste, make balls the size of a walnut. Now add the finely chopped parsley and wrap it around the meatballs. Peel the potatoes and quarter them.

When the lamb pieces and the chickpeas are cooked, add them to the meatballs and the potatoes and put back the lid on the pot and keep simmering for a further 30mns. Check that the potatoes and the meatballs are cooked then let the sauce thicken with the lid off.

On a serving dish place the rice, crown it in the middle with the pieces of lamb. Around the rice align the potatoes and the meatballs. Finally drizzle the sauce on the whole dish. Serve hot.

Kairouan Winter Dish Lamb with Spinach

Serves 4
Cooking time: 1h 30 mins

600g pieces of lamb from the leg = 1.3 lbs
2 medium onions chopped (200g) = 7 oz
3 cloves garlic finely chopped
100g chickpeas (from bottle) = 3.5 oz
3 medium tomatoes chopped (300g) = 10 oz
2 tbsps tomato purée
150g spinach cleaned and roughly chopped = 5.2 oz
1 cup parley chopped = 8 oz
1 tsp cumin
1 tsp sugar
½ tsp *harissa* (or less)
2 tbsps olive oil
Salt and pepper to taste

Grandmother's recipe

In a pot heat the oil, fry the chopped onions and the garlic. When these have been fried add the meat which had been seasoned with salt, pepper and *harissa*. Seal the lamb for 5mns then add the tomato purée and cook for a couple of minutes. Then put the cut up tomatoes, the sugar, the cumin and the chickpeas. Cover with water and check the seasoning. Lower the heat and leave to simmer for 45mns to 1 hour until the meat is very tender. Add the spinach that had been washed and roughly cut as well as the spinach. Simmer for another 10/12mns. Serve hot with mashed potatoes.

Stuffed Beef Sirloin

Serves 4
Cooking time: 1h

750g beef sirloin = 1.65 lbs
150g tuna = 5 oz
1 cup soft bread crumbs
   (50g) = 4.15 oz
¼ cup diced celery (25g)
   = 1 oz
½ medium chopped onion
   (50g) = 3.5 oz
1 tsp butter
1 tsp basil leaves
1 tsp parsley
Salt and pepper to taste

Jamila's recipe

Melt the butter in a small frying pan over low heat. Sauté the onion, celery and the tuna until the onion is soft and transparent about 10mns. Place the bread crumbs in a bowl. Mix in the salt, pepper, basil leaves and parsley. Pour in the butter and onion mixture. Lightly mix until well blended. Make a lengthwise cut, ¾ through the sirloin. Lightly place stuffing in the pocket formed by the cut. Close the pocket by fastening meat together with wooden toothpicks. Place stuffed meat in an oven-proof rectangular baking dish. Bake uncovered in a medium-rare oven 180°C for 30/40mns. Check that it is cooked before serving hot with salad and warm bread.

Tahfifa

Serves 4
Cooking time: 2h 10 mins

500g diced beef = 1 lb 2 oz
750g pumpkin = 1.65 lbs
250g cabbage = 0.55 lb
2 onions finely chopped (200g) = 7 oz
1 cup olive oil (237ml) = 1 cup
½ tsp *harissa*
½ tsp coriander seeds crushed
½ tsp paprika
Salt and black pepper to taste

My friend Jackie's recipe – traditional Jewish beef stew with pumpkin.

In a cooking pot heat the oil and fry the finely chopped onions. Add *harissa*, coriander seeds and the kosher diced beef. Add the paprika, the washed cabbage leaves and the cut up pumpkin. Cover with water and cook on low heat 150°C. Leave to simmer for 2 hours. Ten minutes before the end of the 2 hours with a fork crush the cabbage leaves and the pumpkin into a puree. Leave to reduce for a few minutes. Check the season and serve hot.

Vegetables

P. 147 **Kafteji**

P. 148 **Stuffed Artichokes**

P. 149 **Nabeul Aubergine**

P. 151 **Standard Chakchouka**

P. 153 **Stuffed Tomatoes**

P. 153 **Beja Chakchouka**

P. 154 **Potatoes with Onion and Herbs**

P. 155 **Kairouan Potato Kifta**

P. 157 **Kairouan Koucha**

Kafteji

Serves 4
Cooking time: 40 mins

6 green peppers (750g) = 1.65 lbs
2 medium potatoes (250g) = 7 oz
4 tomatoes (400g) = 14 oz
4 eggs
1 tsp coriander powder
Salt and black pepper to taste
Vegetable oil for frying

Kafteji is basically a food staple, often bought and consumed in the street – what one calls street food. It is said to be Jewish but the "ji" (meaning profession in Turkish) and "kafte" is the kofta – also a Turkish dish. Initially it contained meat but this was expensive and the workers left it out in order to make it a staple food that would be portable and cheap. It is basically the equivalent of a sandwich, but what a delicious rich sandwich! Usually a freshly baked bread fried roll torn (the other meaning of kafte) in which fried potatoes and courgettes, aubergines, tomatoes and pumpkin and inserted with hot *harissa* and spices. Nowadays to make it more de luxe a number of restaurants in Tunisia have *kafteji* on their menu and serve it with beef escalope or some merguez as well. This recipe is thanks to my cousin Mufida Ferchichi.

Heat some vegetable oil in a pan and fry each component separately then set aside. Fry the green peppers and let them cool. Peel the potatoes, dice them and fry them in the oil. Cut the tomatoes in two, spice them with the coriander, salt and black pepper and fry them in the oil. Fry the eggs.

Peel the fried peppers, de-seed them and slice them finely. Peel and chop the tomatoes. If you are preparing the *kafteji* as a food street cut up the eggs finely and mix all the fried vegetables and season. Open the freshly baked bread roll and stuff these inside. Enjoy!

Note: If you are serving the *kafteji* on a plate leave the frying of the egg to the end and make sure it is not overcooked, but more like a poached egg which you place on a bed of mixed vegetables. Serve with freshly baked bread. It is delicious.

Stuffed Artichokes

Serves 4
Cooking time: 1h 10 mins

4 medium artichokes
100g minced meat or rice for vegetarians = 3.5 oz
2 medium eggs
1 medium onion finely chopped (100g) = 3.5 oz
5 tbsps olive oil = ¼ cup,
20g grated Parmesan cheese = ¾ oz
30g parsley finely chopped = Just over 1 oz
1 lemon juice
½ tsp tomato purée
½ tsp coriander
½ tsp paprika
1 cup water = 8 fl oz
Salt and pepper to taste

Janet's recipe

Clean the artichokes taking off the outside leaves. Cut off the top of the artichokes at a point between ½ way and the third from the top. Remove the choke and with a spoon make a hole. Rub the artichokes with the lemon juice to stop them from discolouring. Mix the minced meat (or cooked rice), the parsley and the onion. Add the seasoned garlic of salt, pepper, and coriander. Cook the mixture for 10mns. Take off the heat and leave this to cool. Once cool add the eggs and the cheese to the mixture. Then stuff the artichokes with this mixture. Mix the olive oil, the tomato purée, the paprika and the water. Season: salt and pepper. In an oven-proof dish pour this sauce then place the stuffed artichokes in it. Cook in a medium oven at 180°C for 20-30mns or until the artichokes are cooked but keeping their shape and the sauce not too dry. Serve hot.

Nabeul Aubergine

Serves 4
Cooking time: 2h 20 mins

- 3 medium sized aubergines (1kg) = 2.2 lbs, peeled and sliced 2cm / ¾ inch thick
- 3 medium size onions (300g) = 10.5 oz, peeled and sliced 2 cm / ¾ inch thick)
- 3 medium sized ripe tomatoes (375g) = 0.77 lbs, sliced 2cm / ¾ inch thick)
- 6 cloves garlic crushed
- ¾ cup olive oil (177ml) = 6 fl oz
- 3 tbsps water
- 1 tsp salt or more to taste
- ½ tsp pepper

Naima's recipe

Heat the oil in a large frying pan. Fry the aubergines a few slices at a time, keeping those fried aside. Then in the same oil fry the onions and likewise keep them in a different dish aside. Finally, in the same oil, fry the sliced tomatoes. Make sure you do not burn any one. They need to be soft but not burnt. In an oven-proof dish put a layer of aubergine slices, season with salt, pepper and a bit of the crushed garlic.

Cover the aubergine layer with the tomato slices, also in a layer. Season: salt, pepper and a little more of the crushed garlic. Then cover the tomatoes with a layer of the sliced onions. Again another layer of aubergine slices, season, a layer of tomato slices, season, a layer of onion slices and so forth. Check seasoning and finally sprinkle with water. In an oven marked 180°C cook for 45mns or more until the aubergines are really soft. Serve hot.

Standard Chakchouka

Serves 4
Cooking time: 55 mins

In Tunisia most people have their own recipe for *chakchouka*, a vegetable dish, an equivalent of the French ratatouille using any combination of vegetables. Here one that I like. It uses my friend Amel's recipe.

400g tomatoes seeded and diced = 0.88 lbs = 14 oz
2 green peppers (250g) (seeded and cut into rings) = 0.55 lbs
2 onions (200g), finely chopped = 7 Oz
2 cloves garlic crushed
2 eggs
⅔ tbsp paprika
⅔ tbsp coriander
⅓ cup olive oil (80ml)
½ tsp dried mint
Salt to taste

Fry the onions in the oil for 12-16mns on medium heat. Do not brown them. Add the tomatoes, paprika, garlic, salt and coriander. Cook covered on low heat for 20mn. Add peppers. Cook for a further 10mn. Break the eggs and add them to the pot. Cook for 5mn longer. Sprinkle the dried mint.

Other variations: you can use potatoes instead of eggs, or aubergines or courgettes or shelled green beans. Another variation of *chakchouka* is *ojja*. The difference is instead of coriander use caraway seeds and instead of breaking the eggs whole they have to be mixed at the last couple of minutes of the cooking. This variation has also more possibilities, using meatballs as well or merguez, prawns or squid.

Stuffed Tomatoes

Serves 4
Cooking time: 30 mins

4 medium tomatoes (400g) = 0.88 lbs = 14 oz
100g breadcrumbs = 3.5 oz
3 garlic cloves
2 tbsps olive oil
2 tbsps parsley

Mother's recipe

Cut the tomatoes top off, make a hole and remove the seeds. Chop garlic and parsley. Mix garlic and parsley with breadcrumbs. Fill the tomatoes hole with this mixture. Add the olive oil and season with salt and pepper. Put back the tops so as to protect the mixture. Place in a pan under the grill in a preheated grill to medium for 10 to 15mns, until the tomatoes are soft and the top is browned. Serve hot.

Beja Chakchouka

Serves 4
Cooking time: 1h 10 mins

500g pumpkin = 1 lb 2 oz
250g dried chestnuts = 0.55 lbs
250g raisins = 0.55 lbs
2 tbsps sugar
½ tbsp paprika
4 tbsps olive oil = 2 oz
Salt to taste

This dish is a speciality of the Beja region and adds in raisins and pumpkins for extra flavour.

Put the dried chestnuts to soak for a few hours. Heat the oil. Add the peeled and diced pumpkin, the chestnuts and the salt. Mix and cover with water. Bring to boil, lower the heat and leave it to simmer until the chestnuts are soft. Add the raisins and the sugar. Mix and continue to cook for another 15-20mns.

Potatoes with Onion and Herbs

Serves 4
Cooking time: 45 mins

900g potatoes cut into cubes = 2 lbs
1 red onion sliced (100g) = 3.5 oz
2 cloves garlic crushed
½ cup olive oil (118 ml) = 8 tbsp
1 tsp lemon juice
Fresh thyme,(chopped) = 2 tbsp
Salt and pepper to taste

My recipe

In a pan of boiling salted water cook the potatoes for 10mns. Drain. Heat the oil in a frying pan to which you fry the sliced onion and garlic for 1mn. Add the lemon juice and cook for a further 1-2mns. Add the potatoes and mix well to coat in the oil. Reduce heat, cover and cook for 20-25mns or until the potatoes are tender and a bit brown. Sprinkle the thyme and season with salt and pepper. Serve immediately. It is served in a side dish to accompany delicious lamb chops.

Kairouan Potato Kifta

Serves 4
Cooking time: 30 mins

750g potatoes = 1.65 lbs
2 onions (200g) finely chopped = 7 oz
4 eggs whisked
100g parsley finely chopped = 3.5 oz
4 tbsps flour
1 cup olive oil (237ml) = 8 fl oz
½ tsp black pepper
1 tsp paprika
Salt to taste

Grandmother's recipe

Boil the potatoes in a saucepan of salted water. Peel them and mash them. Add the parsley, onions, black pepper, paprika and the whisked eggs and mix thoroughly. Check the seasoning. Make balls the size of an egg and then flatten them. Dip them in the flour and then fry them in the hot oil. The *kifta* can be eaten as it is or with a tomato sauce or to accompany meat, chicken or fish dishes.

Kairouan Koucha

Serves 4
Cooking time: 1h 10 mins

Stuffed mixed vegetables - Grandmother's recipe

First cook the rice (See recipe for Kairouan chicken , p135). Leave to cool. Meanwhile prepare the vegetables for the stuffing by making a whole in each. In a large bowl mix the rice, egg, paprika, coriander, parsley, garlic, salt and pepper to taste. Stuff the vegetables. Put them in a large baking dish. In an oven 180°C bake for 40 minutes or a little more until cooked. Sprinkle olive oil. Serve hot.

- 4 tomatoes medium size (500g) = 1 lb 2 oz
- 4 green peppers medium size, seeded (500g) = 1 lb 2 oz
- 2 courgettes cut in two for 4 people (400g) 14 oz
- 4 medium size onions (400g) 14 oz
- 4 cloves of garlic crushed
- 150g rice = ¾ cup
- 2 cups water = 2 cups
- 1 tsp salt
- 60g parsley cleaned and finely chopped = ½ cup
- 1 tbsp paprika
- 1 tsp coriander
- 3 tbsps olive oil
- 1 egg
- Salt and pepper to taste

Sweets, Puddings & Drinks

P. 163 **Rfisa**

P. 164 **Pistachio Custard**

P. 164 **Tunis Almond Cake**

P. 165 **Apple Doughnuts**

P. 166 **Qutayef**

P. 167 **Sousse Fresh Melon**

P. 169 **Samsar**

P. 170 **Laklouka from Sfax**

P. 171 **Mhalbiya**

P. 173 **Ghraiba**

P. 173 **Zriga**

P. 175 **Mint Tea with Pine Nuts**

P. 176 **Lemonade**

P. 177 **Rosata**

Sweets Puddings, Drinks

New dishes beget new appetite

One cake eaten in peace is worth two in trouble.

Tunisia is a sweet-loving nation. Sweets and puddings are regarded as family treats and are for celebrating such milestone family events as the arrival of a new baby. During this period the mother is treated by the rest of the family as a princess and receives special care from her husband and the rest of the family. One dessert is *zrir*, a sweet paste made from hazel nuts, sesame and honey, which is recommended for women who are breastfeeding, as it assists lactation. The mother is offered this three times a day. Callers and well-wishers are also served this dish to welcome the newcomer to the world.

Fresh fruits are the main alternative to sugary desserts. Most Mediterranean fruits are sold in the market place in season. Melons and soft fruits such as apricots and peaches are found in summer, grapes in late summer, September to November is the awaited pomegranate season and citrus fruits peak in the early months of the year, although lemons appear all year round. People eat fresh fruit throughout the day and at meal time. They add rose water, cinnamon, sugar, roasted almonds or ice. For instance they take the seeds of 4 pomegranates and mash them, sprinkle them with rose water, lemon juice and sugar to taste and serve them very cold or with ice. For oranges they peel them, slice them and peel the skin off. Dress them on a plate, sprinkle with cinnamon and serve them refrigerated. By the way Thomson oranges are as juicy and tasty as any other genre.

Kairouan Patisserie in Ramadan **(opposite)**.

Sweets

Rfisa

Serves 4
Cooking time: 20 mins

250g couscous = 9 oz = 2 cups
100g caster sugar = 3½ oz
125g raisins = 4½ oz = 1 cup
1 tbsp butter
1 tbsp olive oil (15ml)
½ cup boiling water

My grandmother's recipe - this is a sweet couscous flavoured with raisins.

Mix the couscous with boiling water and the olive oil in a bowl away from the heat and cover so that the couscous absorbs the liquid. Check that the couscous is cooked. If it needs more time or more boiling water, give it a couple of tablespoons more. Add the raisins, the butter and the caster sugar and mix thoroughly. Serve warm.

My grandmother always cooked her couscous in the traditional couscous pot, but it is more time-consuming, so I generally use the simpler method above.

For special occasions she added a tablespoon of each of the following: almonds, walnuts, hazelnuts, pine nuts, pistachio nuts, lemon juice, essence of geranium or rosewater. The nuts would be grilled and grated, and she sometimes replaced the nuts with dates, stoned and diced

Pistachio Custard

Serves 4
Cooking time: 30 mins

½ litre milk = 2 cups = 1 oz
3 egg yolks
125g caster sugar = 1 cup
3 tbsps corn flour
2 tbsps pine nuts
1 tsp grated pistachios
1 tbsp distilled water of geranium

Grandmother's recipe

Mix the milk, the egg yolks, the sugar and the corn flour.

Place in a pan and cook over medium heat stirring all the while until the cream is thick. Add the pine nuts and the essence of geranium or rose water. Continue stirring. Take off the heat and pour into ramekins.

Sprinkle with the grated pistachios. Serve hot or cold.

Tunis Almond Cake

Serves 4
Cooking time: 1h

3 medium eggs
150g ground almonds = 4 lbs 6 oz
150g caster sugar = 4 lbs 6 oz
Zest of 1 orange (4g) = 2½ tbsp
Juice of 1 orange (4 tsps)
2 tbsps of orange blossom water

Alia's recipe

Separate the eggs. Beat the yolks in 130g of the sugar. Fold in the almonds, zest and juice. In another bowl beat the egg whites and add in the 20g of sugar. Mix the whole lot carefully in the liquor. Grease the bottom and sides of a cake-tin 17.5cm (7 inches) in diameter. Add the mixture and cover the top with tin foil. Cook in a pre-heated oven at medium heat (180°C), for 45 minutes. Cool in the tin then turn the cake out. A very similar cake is found in the eastern area of Spain. Using local produce promotes freshness and saves food miles.

Apple Doughnuts

Serves 4
Cooking time: 30 mins

750g apples = 1 lb 10 oz
250g flour = 9 oz
200g sugar = 9 oz
2 tbsps icing sugar (for dusting)
2 eggs
2 tbsps butter
1 sachet baking powder
Oil for frying
A pinch of salt

My neighbour Jamila's recipe

In a large dish make dough with the flour, the baking powder, the pinch of salt, and the melted butter. Mix well then break into this the two eggs and add a little water to produce soft dough.

Wash, cut the apples in equal thickness rings and remove the core.

Put the oil on to heat. When it is piping hot take the apple rings one by one, dip them into the dough and drop them into the oil to deep-fry. Turn them so that they are fried on both sides and golden crisp. Dust with icing sugar. Serve hot.

Qutayef

Serves 4
Cooking time: 55 mins
(plus 1h resting time)

500g angel hair pasta or vermicelli = 1 lb 2 oz
500g caster sugar = 1 lb 2 oz
100g almonds = 3.5 oz
100g hazelnuts = 3.5 oz
100g walnuts = 3.5 oz
60g pine nuts = 4 oz
250g salted butter = 9 oz
1 lemon
2 tbsps geranium essence

Aunt Fatma's recipe - angel hair pasta cake.

In a pot melt the salted butter and then sauté the angel hair pasta for five minutes. Take off the heat.

Blanch the almonds and grill them with the hazelnuts and walnuts. Then crush all nuts and add half of the sugar (250g) to half of the nuts and stir. Butter a 23cm (9 inches) diameter mould. Pour into it a third of the angel hair pasta to make the first layer, followed by half of the mixture of the nuts, followed by another third of the angel hair pasta, followed by the other half of the mixed nuts. Finally pour the last third of the angel hair pasta on top.

Turn the rest of the sugar into syrup, adding the juice of the lemon and the essence of geranium. Put the mould in the oven on a slow heat (150°C) for 30 minutes. Once done, take it out and sprinkle the syrup over the top and leave to stand for 5-7 minutes. Take off the heat add pine nuts and leave to rest the cake for an hour. Then cut the cake into slices and serve.

Sousse Fresh Melon

Serves 4
Cooking time: 20 mins

1½ large melons (1.2kg) = 2 lbs 11 oz
60g walnuts = 4 oz
75g caster sugar = 4.5 oz
1 tbsp sesame seeds
1 tbsp water
Juice of ½ lemon = 1 oz

Our friend Monique's recipe - Sousse fresh melon with caramelized walnuts and sesame seeds.

Quarter the melons, remove the seeds and refrigerate.

Crush the walnut. Pour the sugar into a pan and add the water. Cook these until the sugar caramelises. Stop the cooking process by adding the lemon juice. Take the caramel off heat and add the crushed walnuts.

Pour immediately over the melon and sprinkle with the sesame seeds. Serve.

Samsar

Serves 4
Cooking time: 1h

500g powdered almonds = 1 lb, 2 oz
850g caster sugar = 1 lb 14 oz
2 whole eggs
4 filo pastry sheets
1 tbsp sesame seeds grilled
1 tsp distilled essence of geranium (you can use vanilla essence instead)
5 drops orange water essence
Juice of ½ small lemon (2 tsps)
Oil for frying

Aunt Fatma's recipe – sweet stuffed *brik* with almonds.

To the powdered almonds add half of the caster sugar, the eggs and the orange essence. Mix thoroughly.

Make syrup with the rest of the sugar and the lemon juice. Add the geranium or vanilla essence.

Separate the filo pastry sheets. In the centre of each individual filo pastry sheet put a generous tablespoon of the stuffing. Fold the edges of the filo to make a square then fold diagonally to make a triangle around the stuffing.

Heat the oil and immerse the triangles one at a time to fry them on both sides until golden. Drain. Dip them in the syrup for a few minutes. Place on a serving dish and sprinkle with the sesame seeds. Serve hot or cold.

Laklouka from Sfax

Serves 4
Cooking time: 45 mins

500g raisins (dark and juicy) = 4 cups
125g flour = 1 cup
100ml olive oil= 3.5 oz
125g caster sugar = 1 cup
125g roasted and blanched almonds = 1 cup
100g roasted sesame seeds = 3.5 oz
375ml water = 4 cups

Wash the raisins, dry them and blend to make a paste. Add half the water and keep adding water a bit at a time and kneading the paste. Place the mixture in a fine mesh sieve and push it through the mesh into a bowl so that only the pure paste passes through.

Put the resulting paste in a non-stick pot. Add the sugar and then the olive oil and cook on low heat while mixing all the time with a wooden spoon until the mixture is reduced to half the original quantity and becomes thick like syrup. Take off the heat.

Roast the flour for twenty minutes at 180°C, making sure it is does not burn and then allow to cool. Mix this thoroughly into the raisins paste and return to the fire. Again on low heat keep cooking while mixing all the while. The cooking process should take about 15 minutes. Take off the fire and leave to cool. Make a sausage shape of the dough 2cm (¾ inch) in diameter and cut into 5cm (2 inches) pieces. Make an oval shape of each piece and arrange them on a tray.

Lightly roast the sesame seeds. Sprinkle sesame seeds over the pieces of raisins and flour dough and decorate with one roasted and blanched almond.

Display your cakes artistically on a serving tray. They are ready to be enjoyed.

Mhalbiya

Serves 4
Cooking time: 40 mins

250g short-grain rice = 9 oz
155g sugar = 5½ oz
½ cup geranium water = 4 oz
1¼ cup water = 9 oz
2 cups very hot milk = 1 lb
2 tbsps crushed pistachios
2 tbsps pitted and diced dates

This dish is often served in weddings and festivals. It is a rice pudding dessert dish made from white rice and flavoured with geranium water and vanilla, and topped with crushed pistachios and dates. Some people use orange blossom or rosewater instead of geranium. Rice puddings are popular all over the world – they are cheap to make, easy to prepare, do not take time and above all are healthy. This Tunisian version takes twenty minutes to prepare and a further twenty minutes to cook. So after forty minutes you have a delicious pudding. It is traditionally made with round or ground rice, which can be created at home by running long grain rice in a small food processor until the kernels are small.

Bring the water to the boil. Add the vanilla, sugar and the geranium water and mix well. Cook covered over a very low heat for ten minutes. Then add the very hot milk, a bit at a time and stir all the while. If necessary add a little more very hot milk in order to obtain a texture like a thick porridge.

Remove the pan from the heat. Traditionally it is served in a large bowl, but nowadays Tunisian people serve it in individual pretty dishes and decorate with dates and pistachios.

Ghraiba

Serves 4
Cooking time: 15 mins

500g chickpeas flour = 1 lb 2 oz
125g wheat flour = 1 cup
250g icing sugar = 9 oz
250g butter melted over bain marie = 9 oz

My grandmother's recipe. This is a kind of shortbread but made from chickpea flour. It melts in the mouth. When I was a little girl I preferred it to baklava.

Mix both flours with the sugar. Pour in the melted butter and mix thoroughly. You then have a rather hard dough. To soften the dough and make it easily manageable for kneading, mix it further in a blender. Then work it with your fingers and make a firm sausage about 4cm (1½ inches) in diameter. With a knife, cut diagonally to make little diamonds cakes. Score each four times across the top.

Cover a tray with grease proof paper and place the diamonds on it. Heat the oven to 180°C and put them in to bake for five minutes. Watch that they do not burn. They should look slightly yellow and similar, in fact to how they look when they went in. Do not leave too long or they will be hard and not pleasant to eat. Do not handle them until they are cold, otherwise they will fall into pieces. Place them in a hermetically sealed container. They are so good that one is tempted to eat the whole lot in one go – don't, of course!

Zriga

Serves 4
Cooking time: 1h

500g semolina = 4 cups
100-200g sugar depending on how sweet tooth =3½ – 7 oz
125ml olive oil = ½ cup
1 tbsp salted butter

A Tozeur Breakfast meal.

Mix the semolina and salt and add enough warm water, little by little, until you have a dough, as for bread. Leave to rest for 30 minutes. Then make thin pancakes. Put them in the oven to cook for 10–15 minutes. Leave to cool and then crumble into pieces. Pour over this bread crumble the half cup of olive oil, the tablespoon of salted butter and stir in enough warm water to get a thick porridge. Add sugar to taste. Serve as breakfast.

Mint Tea with Pine Nuts

Serves 4
Cooking time: 12 mins

No special occasion ends without mint tea served with pine nuts. This delicious tea is also served in cafés all over the country. Its sweetness is balanced by the earthiness of the pine nuts.

¼ – ⅓ cup of sugar = 1½ oz
4 tbsps of roasted pine nuts
1 handful fresh mint leaves (30g) = 1 oz
950ml water = 4 cups
1 tbsp loose leaf green tea

In a small saucepan bring the water to a boil. Remove the pan from the heat, add the tea, sugar and stir. Off the heat add the mint and let the tea steep for 5-8 minutes. Strain the tea to remove the mint and the tea leaves. Serve warm in small glasses with one tablespoon of the roasted pine nuts in each glass. Tunisians have special small glasses for serving tea. Unlike British porcelain tea sets, Tunisians ones are made of glass, sometimes coloured, cut or heavily decorated.

Lemonade

Serves 4
Cooking time: 45 mins (+ 5h in fridge before serving)

600g lemons = 1lb 5 oz
125g sugar = 1 cup
237ml water = 1 cup= 8oz
2 l water to dilute =10 cups = 5 pints
2 tbsps orange blossom water

Lemonade can be traced back to medieval Egypt. Although the fruit is believed originally to come to us from India, the first written evidence of this summer drink was found in Egyptian records written by the Persian poet and traveller Nasir-I-Khusraw. It is a refreshing drink enjoyed by all people of all ages all over the world. It is a natural, vitamin rich thirst quencher. Some countries add mint leaves, while others mix it with oranges. The Tunisian variety is fruity and its preparation is labour intensive. It uses the whole fruit including the zest, but removes the pith and seeds. This gives it more body than other varieties. Tunisian lemonade also adds orange blossom water (for which rose water can be substituted, if desired). Most cafés and restaurants serve lemonade with crunchy almonds on the side because both are much loved by Tunisians.

Wash the lemons and cut off both ends. Collect zest from the peel of the lemons. Cut the lemons into thin slices. Be sure to remove seeds and pith which taste bitter and can spoil the taste. Place the zest and the sugar in a saucepan and pour 1 cup of water over it. Mix thoroughly and bring to a boil over a high heat. Lower the heat and simmer for twenty minutes. Add the slices of lemons and continue simmering for a further ten minutes. When all the water has been absorbed, pour the mixture into a blender. Add the orange blossom water and five cups of cold water. Blend again at high speed for a couple of minutes. Place in the fridge for at least five hours. Pass the mixture through a fine sieve. Add the remaining five cups of water mixing well.

Before serving taste that the lemonade is not too sweet. Adding water a little at a time so that you get the right sweetness and consistency for you. The lemonade needs to be served very cold with a slice of lemon for decoration stuck on the edge of the glass.

Rosata

Serves 4
Cooking time: 10 mins (and leave overnight before serving)

135g ground blanched almonds = 1 cup
120g sugar = 1 cup
1 tbsp almond extract
1 tbsp vanilla extract
1½ l water = 2 cups

This is a delicious cold drink which is made from peeled almonds and has its origin in Ottoman Empire. It is served as an aperitif.

For those of you who read *Colette's Gigi*, **or saw the film, you may remember how her old aunt cupped her hands over Gigi's breasts and made her promise 'not to eat too many almonds, because they make the bosom large'. How things changed! Here is a recipe to make rosata:**

In a large pot put the ground blanched almonds in 1½ litres of water and the sugar. Cook for 5 to 10mns until the sugar is dissolved. Drain and leave in the fridge overnight. Just before serving flavour with the almond and vanilla extract. Serve in attractive glasses.

Pickles & Breads

P. 180 **Hot Peppers**

P. 180 **Eggplants**

P. 181 **Turnips**

P. 185 **Kairouan Bread**

P. 185 **Tunis Bread**

P. 187 **Mabsout**

Hot Peppers

Serves 4
Cooking time: 10 mins
(and 10 days later serve)

To pickle 500g of these in a jar: Choose small hot peppers. Trim them and put them with two teaspoons of salt and fill the rest of the jar with white vinegar. Wait at least ten days before serving.

500g small hot peppers = 1 lb 2 oz
2 tsps salt
White vinegar for the rest of the jar

Eggplants

Serves 4
Cooking time: 10 mins
(and 10 days later serve)

Choose small eggplants (aubergines) and a jar big enough for the eggplants all to fit in it. Wash, trim and boil the eggplants for few minutes. When cold, slit the eggplants open and stuff with garlic and salt. Place then in the jar and fill with one third vinegar and two thirds water. Leave for ten days before serving.

500g of small eggplants = 1 lb 2 oz
2-3 cloves of garlic to taste
2 tspsof salt
Vinegar for the rest of the jar

Turnips

Serves 4
Cooking time: 10 mins
(and 10 days later serve)

500g small turnips = 1.1 lbs
237ml vinegar = 1 cup
475ml water = 2 cups
2 tspsof salt
2-3 cloves of garlic
1 beetroot (optional)
   (100g) = 3.5oz

Choose small turnips, peel and cut in quarters. Soak them in water overnight. The next day place them in a glass jar with two teaspoons of salt, the vinegar and the water. A whole beetroot is sometimes added to add colour to the pickled turnips and also cloves of garlic (quantity depends on individual tastes). These can be served after only three days. The same recipe can be used to pickle carrots, just swap the turnips for carrots or radishes and proceed as above.

Breads

'Eating bread will broaden your shoulders.'

Bread provides energy for daily living. Carbohydrates are an important part of our diet as they provide with energy B vitamins. It is also better for you, pound for pound, than white rice. Its protein and fibre content fills you fuller for longer than white rice. It also increases your metabolic rate. Bread can be an ingredient in other culinary preparations – using crumbs to add crunch to crusts or thicken sauces, or adding croutons to soups and salads, while seasoned bread stuffs chicken or lamb dishes.

Bread is eaten with every meal, an essential accompaniment to Tunisian cuisine. It is usually used for dipping -ideally still warm from the local bakery. Some aromatic plants are added to the bread, such as thyme, cinnamon or pepper. On special occasions and feasts such as Ramadan and Eid several types of bread can be found on the table. Members of the family buy their personal favourites. A French style baguette is the standard loaf, but often in the countryside traditional Berber bread flat, round and subtly flavoured with aniseed, is favoured. Kairouan is famous for its range of bread. Sousse is known for its Italian style breads, while Sfax has its own *mabsout*.

Opposite: It is some 2,000 years since the lands of North Africa were the luscious bread baskets of the Roman Empire, but Tunisia still has much fertile land providing grain. Seen here is a stone mill probably very little changed in design over the past few thousand years.

Tunis Bread

Kairouan Bread

Serves 4
Cooking time: 1h 45 mins

750g flour = 6 cups
530ml tepid water = 2¼ cups
30g sugar = 2 oz
1 packet yeast (7g, ¼oz)
1 tsp salt
2 tbsps olive oil

Aunt Fatma's recipe.

In a large bowl pour the yeast into the tepid water with a pinch of sugar. The yeast will shortly froth up slightly, at which point add the oil, the rest of the sugar and four cups of the flour. Mix thoroughly until you get dough. Keep adding a half cup of flour at intervals, mixing continually until you get dough that sticks. Knead for five to seven minutes.

Make a ball and put it in an oiled bowl. Turn the dough over in the bowl order to coat it in oil and cover the bowl with cling film. Leave to rest for an hour until it doubles its size. Divide the dough into two halves. Roll each half into a rectangle of 20cm / 8 inches long and 10cms / 4 inches wide). Do the same with the second half. Put the bread in a lightly oiled bread mould. Cover it with cling-film and leave to rest for one hour. Preheat the oven to 190 C. Put the bread and cook for 30-35mns.

Tunis Bread

Serves 4
Cooking time: 1h 35 mins

450g plain flour = 1 lb
2 small pots natural yoghurt (200g) = 7 oz
3 eggs of which 1 with yolk removed to prepare the crust
1½ small packets of yeast (each 7g, ¼oz)
2 tsps seeds (1 black and 1 white) to taste
1 tsp salt

Amal recipe
This recipe comes from Amal Kechrid, a medical doctor and a superb cook who comes from Sfax and studied in Tunis where she lives married to Ridha, a surgeon from Kairouan, and ex-Ambassador to Spain.

Mix all the ingredients. Leave an hour to double in size. Then shape the bread as you want it. Brush with egg yolk and place in a preheated oven at 190°C for 30/35mns.

Mabsout

Serves 4
Cooking time: 1h 10 mins

500g semolina = 1 lb 2 oz
25gr yeast = 1 oz
½ tbsp sesame seeds
½ tbsp nigella or cumin seeds
½ tsp salt

This small semolina flatbread from Sfax uses nigella seeds, replaceable by cumin seeds.

Make bread dough with the semolina, salt, yeast and enough water for a normal dough. Leave the dough an hour or so (depending on the season) to rise. Knead the dough and divide it into four equal parts to make small flat breads. Dust with the sesame and cumin seeds. Place in a heavy frying pan, with oil preheated. Cook both sides of the bread until golden, usually around 7 minutes each side.

In other parts of the Sfax region and in Beja, *tabouna* bread, which is very popular everywhere, is baked in small flatbread format using barley instead of flour. It follows the same recipe as *mabsout*, and is called *jradaq*.

GLOSSARY

Asida: A breakfast pudding made with flour or semolina, oil and dates.
Baklava: Layers of thin pastry interspersed with ground pine nuts, almonds, pistachios, hazelnuts, brushed in golden butter, baked and dipped in a honey syrup.
Barkoukech: A Southern 'pot-au-feu' using three meats: beef or lamb, chicken and fish.
Basra: A city in Iraq and its main port, from which the fictional Sinbad the Sailor sailed. It played an early role in Islamic history.
Beja: Town in Tunisia
Bizerta: Town in Tunisia
Brik A triangular pocket of deep-fried puff pastry with a variety of fillings, with an egg cooked inside. Name derived from the Turkish 'Boreik'.
Broudou: Thick soup.
Bsisa: Breakfast cereal.
Chakchouka: Spicy Tunisian ratatouille equivalent.
Chorbat frik: Green wheat, an oily, tomato-based soup with a punch.
Convivencia: Coexistence - the relative peace enjoyed in the Muslim kingdoms of Spain between Muslims, Christians and Jews down to 1492.
Fermess: Type of dried apricots from the Gafsa region.
Fricassé: A popular small sandwich with tuna, *harissa*, olives and olive oil, served in restaurants throughout the day and evening.
Gafsa: Oasis town in Tunisia'
Hab hlaoua: Aniseed.
Halal: Meaning 'permissible in Muslim law'. It is the way to slaughter animals and birds for cooking permitted by the Koran, like kosher in the Jewish faith.
Harissa: Hot ready-made chili peppers and garlic paste used to spice many dishes.
Hlelem: Thin hand-rolled noodles for soup.
Horchata: A Spanish summer drink of soaked, ground and sweetened tiger nuts.
Hsou: Spicy semolina and caper-based soup
Ifrikiya: Is the Roman name for the lands of Algeria, Tunisia and Libya.
Jradaq: Flat bread
Kafteji: A sandwich of vegetables and egg. restaurants now serve them on a plate.
Kammouniya: Octopus dish using cumin powder. If it is bil quarnit, it has lots of cumin.
Keskes: Colander style utensil for steaming couscous and other cereals.
Khobz Tabouna: Traditional oven-baked bread. It is not flat like pita bread.
Kufa: A city in Iraq. Its Great Mosque is one of the earliest and holiest surviving mosques in the world built in the 7th century.
kufa: shopping basket made of cane and straw.
Lablabi: Rich vegetarian soup with chickpeas, popular all over Tunisia.
La Goulette: The fishing port suburb of the capital, Tunis –a centre for fish and seafood.

Le Kram: A suburb of Tunis
Laklouka: A traditional pastry cake with raisins, sesame seeds, sugar and olive oil.
Maaquouda: Fried mashed potato cake/fritter, bought as street food, sometimes served as a snack in a bread roll with salad, or as a side dish.
Mabsout: Bread using nigella seeds. It is a specialty from Sfax.
Malsuqa: Paper thin puff pastry used in cakes and some savoury dishes.
Malthouth: A kind of couscous dish from the southern town of Sfax.
Mdammis: Dried white bean soup.
Mhamas: Large couscous, with pellets the size of dry chickpeas, are rubbed in olive oil, steamed for an hour, then added to a favourite Tunisian sauce.
Makroudh: Semolina cake stuffed with dates or almonds, cinnamon and grated orange, and peel, diamond shape. It is a specialty of Kairouan.
Masfouf: Sweetened couscous served as a desert with milk and little honey at sundown in Ramadan.
Merguez: Small spicy lamb sausages.
Mhalbiya: Cake made with rice, nuts and geranium water.
Molokhiyeh: A dish mainly based on a member of the spinach family.
Mrayish: A Beja chicken piece speciality, cooked in broth, served on pancake crumbs.
Nhassa: Stew pot below the keskes where the sauce of the couscous is cooked.
Ojja: Scrambled egg dish made of tomatoes and mild green chillies, *Harissa* and dried meats or merguez.
Omok houria: A delicious carrot puree salad, a favourite in all times.
Osban: Offal made into meatballs and wrapped in sheep's stomach, a speciality from Monastir.
Qaddid: Dried meat.
Ras el hanout: A mixture of black pepper, rose petals and cinnamon.
Rechta: Is a type of noodles that is prepared with meat or chicken cooked in vegetable sauce and flavoured with cinnamon.
Samsa: Small sweet samosa shaped cakes, stuffed with nuts and dipped in sweet syrup.
Slata mechouia: Grilled salad.
Slatat blankit: French baguette salad.
Slatit Fondoq il ghalla: Mixed vegetable market salad.
Smen: Clarified butter.
Sohleb: Sweetened sorghum flour sold in winter all over Tunisia.
Tabil: Mixed dried and ground spices - coriander, caraway, garlic and cayenne pepper.
Tabouna: Berber flat bread made in a traditional clay oven.
Zlebia: A sweet Catherine wheel shape light fritter dipped in sugar syrup.

FURTHER READING

Dozy, Reinhard – *Le Calendrier de Cordoue de L'Annee 961' - Texte Arabe et Ancienne Traduction Latine*. E.J. Brill, 1873.
Kouki, Mohamed – *La Cuisine Tunisienne d'Omok Sannafa*. S.A.E.P., 1967.
Fletcher, Richard – *The Quest for El Cid*. New York: Alfred A. Knopf, 1990.
Boulares, Habib. *History of Tunisia' From Prehistory to Revolution*. Ceres Editions, 2011.
Lelouch, Jacob – *Lettres de la Noblesse de la Gastronomie Tunisienne*. Ceres Bookshop, 2019.
Muasher, Marwan – *The Second Arab Awakening*. Yale University Press, 2014.
Rossi, Pierre. *La Tunisie de Bourguiba*. Editions Kahia, 1967.
Monod, Theodore – *Les deserts*. Horizons de France, 1973.
Trustees of Dt George's Church, The. *At Home in Carthage: The British in Tunisia*. Tunis 1992.
Driss, Abdelaziz – *Tresors du Musee National du Bardo*. S.T.D. Tunis, 1966.
Chabbouh, Ibrahim.Kairouan – *A travers les Cartes Postales 1895-1940*. Les Editions de la Mediterranee, 2009.
Pliny the Elder – *Natural History*. Rome, 70-72 BC.
Daoulatli, Abdelaziz – *Tunisia' Land of Enchantment*. Plurigraf Italia, 1990.
Roy, ClaudeSebag, Paul – *Tunisie' De Carthage à Demain*. Paris: Delpire, 1961.
Turki, Zubeir – *Tunis' Nageure et Aujourd'hui* Adapted in French by Claude Roy. Tunis: Ministry
of Information and Tourism.
Fletcher, Richard – *Moorish Spain*. Phoenix, 2001.
Tolan, J. and Veinstein, G. and Laurens, H. *Europe and the Islamic World: A History*. Princeton, 2016.
Dr Dharma Singh Khalsa – Food As Medicine, Pullman, USA 2011

INDEX

Almonds, 41, 42, 133, 164, 166, 171, 170, 177
Anchovy salad, 109
Apples:
    Apple doughnuts, 165
    Tunisian salad, 102
Apricots: 81
Artichokes, 61, 113, 148
    Stuffed artichokes, 148
Baguette, 105, 107
Baking powder, 39, 44, 165
Baklava, 42
Barkoukech, 81
Beans, 81, 83, 93
Beetroot - radish salad 108
Beja Chakchouka, 153
Bey's baklava, 42
Beef & Beef
    Barkoukech (very thick couscous dish), 81
    Dried beef, 87
    Jewish beef stew with pumpkin, 143
    Soup: shorbat frik, 36
    Stewing steak beef & tomato macaroni, 95
    Stuffed beef sirloin, 142
    Beef with macaroni, 93
Boucha/vodka - Fricassée 111
Breadcrumbs, 122, 124, 142, 153
Bread:
    Fish stew, 123
    Mabsout, 187
    Tunis bread, 185:
Butter, 39, 42, 50, 68, 76, 79, 134, 136, 142, 163, 165, 173
Butternut squash, 52, 143
Cabbage, 50, 76, 143
Capers:
    Anchovy salad, 109
    Fish stew, 123
    Chicken tajin, 66
    Slata Mechouia, 100
    Slatit Blankit, 105
    Slatit Fondouq El Ghalla, 113
Carrots, 53, 76, 80, 81, 113, 132
Cauliflowers, 61, 71
Celery, 36, 76, 81, 87, 142
Chard, 81
Cheeses,
    Edam, 68, 113
    Gruyère, 68, 93, 105, 107, 134
    Parmesan, 61, 68, 71, 93
Chicken:
    Chicken briks, 60
    Chicken couscous, 52
    Chicken tajin, 66
    Chicken in oven with rice, 134
    Chicken with almond sauce, 133
    Chicken with pistachios, 41
    Stuffed chicken, 130
    Tajin malsouka, 68
    Walnut chicken, 132

Whole chicken soup, 76
Chickpeas, 36, 50, 52, 53, 66, 68, 81, 82, 84, 92, 138
Courgettes, 52, 121
Couscous:
    Fish couscous, 50
    Chicken couscous, 52
    Kairouan Makroudh, 39
    Lamb couscous, 54
    Rfisa, 163
Dates:
    Makroudh, 39
    Mhalbiya, 171
Dried chestnuts - Beja Chakchouka 153
Edam, 68, 113
Egg briks, 59
Fennel Salad, 109
Filo pastry/malsouka:
    Baklava, 42
    Chicken briks, 60
    Egg briks, 59
    Samsar, 169
    Tajin malsouka, 68
Fish:
    Broudou, 80
    Couscous, 50
    Poisson complet, 121
    Soup, 79
    stew, 123
Flour:
    Apple doughnuts, 165
    Fricassée, 111
    Ghraiba, 173
    Kairouan bread, 185
    Kairouan makroudh, 39
    Potato Kifta, 155
    Tunis bread, 185
    Vegetable cakes, 61
    Zlebia, 44
Fricassée, 111
Frisa, 163
Garlic: 36, 76, 81, 82, 83, 84, 93, 95, 114, 121, 122, 123, 125, 133, 138, 140, 149, 151, 153, 154, 157
Ghraiba, 173
Green salad/lettuce:
    Poisson complet 121
Green tea, 175
Gruyère: 68, 93, 105, 107, 134
Harissa: 52, 53, 70, 71, 82, 83, 84, 87, 105, 107, 111, 112, 124, 125, 138, 140, 143
Hazelnuts, 42, 166
Hlelem, 87
Honey:
    Bey's baklava, 42
    Makroudh, 40
    Zlebia, 44
Kale:
    Fish broudou, 80
Kairouan:

bread, 185
Makroudh, 39
Kifta - Potato, 155
Koucha, 133
Lablabi, 84
Laklouka, 170
Lamb:
   couscous, 54
   cutlets, 135
   leg of lamb with artichokes, 136
   meatballs, 138
   with spinach, 140
Leeks, 80
Lemonade, 176
Lemons/lemon juice:
   Bey's baklava, 42
   Chicken briks, 60
   Egg briks, 59
   Fennel salad, 109
   Fish soup, 79
   Fresh melon, 167
   Fricassée, 111
   Koucha, 133
   Lablabi, 84
   Laklouka 170
   Lamb cutlets, 135
   Leg of lamb with artichokes, 136
   Lemonade, 176
   Makroudh, p,40
   Mhalbiya, 171
   Potatoes with onions & herbs, 154
   Slata mechouia, 100
   Radish salad, 109
   Samsar, 169
   Slatit fondouq il Ghalla, 112 & 113
   Stuffed artichokes, 148
   Zlabia, 44
Mabsout, 187
Macaroni:
   In the oven, 93
   With beef & tomato, 95
Makroudh, 39, 40
Melons, 167
Merguez, 87
Mhalbiya, 171
Milk:
   Mhalbiya, 171
   Pistachio custard, 164
Mincemeat:
   Lamb meatballs, 138
   Stuffed artichokes, 148
   Stuffed chicken, 130
Mint tea with pine nuts, 175
Nuts:
   Almonds, 42, 42, 133, 164, 166, 169, 170, 177
   Hazelnuts, 42, 166
   Pine nuts 130, 164, 166, 175
   Pistachios, 41, 42, 164, 171
   Walnuts, 44, 132, 166, 167
Olives (black & green), 100, 102, 105, 107, 108, 109, 111, 113
Oranges - Tunis almond cake, 164
Parmesan, 61, 68, 71, 93
Peas, 113
Pine nuts, 130, 164, 166, 175
Pistachios, 41, 42, 164, 171

custard, 164
Potato:
   Kifta, 155
   with, onions & herbs 155
Pumpkin:
   Fricassée, 112
   Tahfifa, 143
   Beja Chakchouka, 153
Qadid & merguez, 87
Qutayef, 166
Radish salad, 108
Raisins:
   Beja Chakchouka, 153
   Fish stew, 123
   Frisa, 163
   Laklouka, 170
Rice:
   Chicken with almond sauce, 133
   Meatballs, 138
   Mkhalbiya, 171
   Rice in the oven with chicken, 134
   Stuffed chicken, 130
Rfisa, 163
Rosata, 177
Samsar, 169
Semolina:
   Mabsout, 187
   Zriga, 173
Slatit Blankit, 105
Slatit Fondouq El Ghalla, 113
Slata mechouia, 100
Smen (clarified butter):
   Makroudh, 39
Spinach, 68, 140
Tahfifa, 143
Tajin malsouka, 68
Tea:
   Green tea, 175
   Mint tea with pine nuts, 175
Tunis almond cake, 164
Tunis bread, 185
Tunisian salad, 102
Turnips, 52, 53, 76, 80, 81
Beef kidneys - Tajin malsouka, 68
Vegetable cakes, 61
Vermicelli/angel hair pasta - Qutayef 166
Vinegar, 102, 105, 107, 109, 180, 181
Walnuts, 42, 132, 166, 167
Wheat:
   Cracked wheat/borghol, 82
   Green wheat/frik,36
Yeast, 44, 111, 185, 187
Yoghurt, 185
Zlebia, 44
Zriga,173

About the Author

Hafida Ben Rajeb Latta

Hafida Ben Rejeb Latta was born in Kairouan in 1944 and was brought up in the house of her grandfather, the late writer, poet and social reformer, Salah Souissi Al Sharif Al Quayrawani.

Her childhood in the company of her widowed mother, grandmother and invalid aunt, unencumbered by male presence, gave her an acute interest in two different loves: academic knowledge at school, and the oxygen of family life represented by all aspects of food. Hafida shopped from an early age, her grandmother cooked and they all sat around eating and talking about food, tastes, aromas, spices and the health benefits of the various ingredients. She still remembers the pride people took in exchanging recipes, which were shared, cherished and passed down generations like an inheritance.

Hafida went on to marry a British diplomat and found herself living on the international merry-go-round of diplomatic life where the tastes and aromas of food brought back familiar comparisons and contrasts with the experiences of her childhood. So she joined every women's group and club she came across: from Karachi (Pakistan) to Beirut (Lebanon) and from Amman (Jordan) to Alcossebre (Spain). And she continued to study, compile and compare the diets and recipes she encountered. *A Daughter of Kairouan* tells stories of her travels, different cultures encountered and life as an expat.

Hafida's lifelong love of food, her experience of international cuisine and above all her appreciation of the Mediterranean culinary traditions has inspired her to create this book - a celebration of healthy eating and all the traditions that surround it.